William Tappan

Pope's Translation of Homer's Iliad

Books I, VI, XXII, XXIV. Vol. 1

William Tappan

Pope's Translation of Homer's Iliad
Books I, VI, XXII, XXIV. Vol. 1

ISBN/EAN: 9783337240394

Printed in Europe, USA, Canada, Australia, Japan

Cover: Foto ©Thomas Meinert / pixelio.de

More available books at **www.hansebooks.com**

HOMER'S ILIAD

EPIC POETRY: HOMER HAILED BY THE ILIAD AND ODYSSEY.

From the mural painting by Puvis de Chavannes in the
Boston Public Library.

POPE'S

TRANSLATION OF

HOMER'S ILIAD

BOOKS I VI XXII XXIV

EDITED

WITH INTRODUCTION AND NOTES

BY

WILLIAM TAPPAN

BOSTON, U.S.A.

GINN & COMPANY, PUBLISHERS

The Athenæum Press

1898

PREFACE.

THE principal aim in this edition of a portion of Pope's *Iliad* has been to present a correct text, with such introduction and commentary as are needed by pupils in secondary schools for a reasonably thorough appreciation of the poem.

The first requisite is an unblemished text; for no amount of commentary or of well-constructed tables can compensate for the harm done by a careless and inaccurate text. It has not, of course, been deemed advisable to retain the obvious errors and vagaries in spelling and punctuation found in the earliest editions. Moreover, some other changes have been made in orthography, to conform to present usage. The following classes of forms have been discarded: the elided verb form in *-y'd*, as *unbury'd, reply'd*, etc.; the form in *-ck* of such words as *public, majestic*, etc.; the preterit and participle in *-t* of verbs ending in an *s* sound, as *addrest, crost, fixt*, etc. For the last-named class the elided form, which was common at the time, has been given, as *address'd, cross'd, fix'd*. The following, also, found in early editions, have been rejected: *'midst, 'till, oft', yon'; cou'd, shou'd, wou'd; e'er* (when used for *ere*); *aukward, battel, cawl, chace, chearful and chearless, controul, croud, dazling, rouze, suspence, traytor*. Those words which good writers in England of the present day would generally spell in -*our*, such as *honour*, *labour*, *splendour*, are so spelled in the text here ; the following are spelled in -*or* : *superior*, *terror*, *warrior*. In other respects, the earliest editions have been followed, and it is believed that an accurate text is offered.

In the matter of annotation, it has been the aim to avoid the fault of over-editing, in the belief that in general a book well worth reading can speak best for itself. What Pope himself has said in the Preface to his *Iliad*, though spoken with reference to one who would essay to translate Homer, applies with equal force to the reader of any masterpiece. "What I would further recommend to him," says Pope, "is to study his author rather from his own text than from any commentators, how learned soever, or whatever figure they may make in the estimation of the world." It is not to be presumed that the pupils who use this book can, in every case, study Homer "from his own text"; but they can study Pope. And through Pope they can form at least a slight acquaintance with Homer; for, as Professor Wilson truly expressed it, "That man is not ignorant of Homer who has read, even in translation, the First Book of the *Iliad*."

Boston, July 24, 1897.   W. T.

CONTENTS.

INTRODUCTION.

HOMER: THE ILIAD.

UNTIL comparatively recent times, it was almost universally assumed that the *Iliad* and *Odyssey*, like the *Aeneid* or *Paradise Lost*, were the work of one author. In 1795, Friedrich August Wolf, a famous German scholar, published his *Prolegomena ad Homerum*, in which he set forth the claim that neither the *Iliad* nor the *Odyssey* was the work of one author ; but that each had consisted originally of a number of separate poems or lays, composed at different times by different men, and that these separate poems had at a later period been collected and arranged in such a way as to give them a unity. This Homeric Question has been the subject of a great deal of discussion ; but it is one with which only critical scholarship is concerned. While most persons competent to form an opinion on the matter now accept the view of a diversity of authorship, still Homer is the name that has always stood, and doubtless will continue to stand, for the authorship of the two great epics.

The *Iliad* and *Odyssey*, which were probably in essentially their present form as early as the eighth century B.C., are the oldest remains of Greek literature, and give us the earliest picture we have of Hellenic life and civilization. Moreover, they have always been regarded as the finest epic poems of the world. The unanimity with which all ages have conceded this place to the Homeric poems seems

to indicate that the experiences and feelings common to the
whole race find in them their truest expression. "The
capital distinction of Homeric poetry," says Professor Jebb,
"is that it has all the freshness and simplicity of a primitive
age, — all the charm which we associate with the 'childhood
of the world'; while, on the other hand, it has completely
surmounted the rudeness of form, the struggle of thought
with language, the tendency to grotesque or ignoble modes
of speech, the incapacity for equable maintenance of a high
level, which belong to the primitive stage in literature." It
has much in common with the early ballad, on the one hand,
and with the literary epic, such as the *Paradise Lost*, on the
other; but it is quite as distinct from the one as from the
other.

It would be idle to expect to find in the *Iliad* an accurate
narrative of historical occurrences; and yet, in a very important — perhaps the most important — sense, the poem has
a substantial historical basis. We may not suppose that
there lived persons named Priam and Hector, Achilles,[1]
Agamemnon, and Helen, who performed the deeds ascribed
to them. But the excavations of Schliemann and others
have aided in showing pretty clearly that there were such
cities as Homer describes; and that his pictures of their
civilization, their art, their dress, their manners, religion,
and government, are remarkably accurate. It is even
probable that about the period 1200–1000 B.C. there
were frequent conflicts between the people of the Troad[2]
and those of Hellas; and there is certainly nothing unrea-
sonable in supposing that there may have been, about that
time, such an invasion as that which the *Iliad* represents
Agamemnon to have led.

Homer's conception of the world is that of a circular
plane bounded by the river Oceanus.[3] The part of this

[1] A-chĭl'-lēṣ.   [2] Trō'-ad.   [3] Ō-çē'-a-nus.

plane known to Homer includes a very limited portion of
the country about the eastern shores of the Mediterranean.
The two leading states of historical Greece, — Athens and
Sparta, — are comparatively insignificant in Homer. The
chief city is Mycenae,[1] whose king is Agamemnon. Homer
uses no one word for the Greeks; they are Argives,[2]
Achaeans,[3] or Danaans.[4]

Democracies are apparently not known; while, on the
other hand, the absolute monarchies of the Tigris-Euphrates
region seem to be equally unknown. The powers of the
Homeric king are limited. He is the supreme judge, acts
as chief priest in public sacrifices and as president of the
council and the assembly, and in time of war commands
the army.

There is a council of elders, and a popular assembly; in
the latter, however, the people seem to have only the right
of expressing approval or dissent. In the *Iliad*, the whole
army constitutes the assembly. In the siege of Troy,
Agamemnon, the most powerful king, is commander-in-chief
of all the Greek forces, the other kings (or chiefs) consti-
tuting a council similar to that of the elders in local government.

The government among the gods is a similar monarchy,
with Zeus[5] (Jupiter) at the head, mightier than all the
others. Athene[6] (Minerva) and Apollo are next in impor-
tance, the former being especially active in war, while Ares[7]
(Mars), the later war-god, is not particularly belligerent or
imposing. The gods dwell in houses built by Hephæstus[8]
(Vulcan) on the summit of Mount Olympus. Sacrifices
constitute the means of worship; temples are rare. The
gods are not free from the vices of men.

---

[1] Mȳ-çē'-naē.   [4] Dăn'-a-ans.   [7] Ā'-rēṣ.

[2] Ar'-ġīves.   [5] Zeūs (*monosyllable*).

[3] A-chaē'-ans.   [6] A-thē'-nē.   [8] He-phæs'-tus (-phĕs'-).

The warriors carry both defensive and offensive armor. The former consists of helmet, cuirass, greaves, belt, and shield ; the latter of spear and sword. The war-chariot, with room for driver and knight, is used for the transportation of the latter, and not for the destruction of the enemy.

Such, in brief, is the background of the *Iliad*. The story itself covers a short period in the siege of Troy, though it will be well to see what led up to the war.

When Peleus[1] and the goddess Thetis were married, all the gods were bidden to the feast except Eris (Discord). To revenge herself for the slight, Eris threw among the guests a golden apple, inscribed " For the fairest." Hera (Juno), Athene (Minerva), and Aphrodite[2] (Venus), each claimed the apple. Zeus shirked the responsibility of deciding the matter, and sent the three claimants to Mt. Ida. Here Paris (Alexander), son of Priam, king of Troy, was tending his flocks : to him the goddesses appealed for a decision, each endeavoring to win by the promise of reward. Venus won by the promise that he should have the fairest of women for his wife. The fairest of women, Helen, was the wife of another, — Menelaüs,[3] king of Sparta. Paris, therefore, under guidance of the goddess, sailed to Greece, where he was hospitably entertained at the court of Menelaüs, whose wife he carried away with him. Now, Helen before her marriage had had many suitors ; and these had made an agreement among themselves, before her decision was known, that they would all maintain the rights of her husband, if it should ever be necessary. Therefore, when she was carried off to Troy, the chieftains of Greece were called upon to aid in her recovery. Ten eventful years were consumed in the preparations : and then the Greeks, a hundred thousand strong, set sail in about twelve hundred ships.

[1] Pē'-leūs.
[2] A-phrō-dī'-tē.
[3] Men-e-lā'-us.

So large a force of men must, of course, give much care to the question of provisions. During the long siege, therefore, they make many expeditions against neighboring towns, obtaining captives and supplies. The siege cannot be pressing at all times ; and the Trojans send out and gain as allies many friendly tribes. For ten years the siege continues, exhausting the strength of the city and well-nigh the hopes of the Greeks. The camp of the latter is at a considerable distance from the city, and the fighting takes place in the plain between the two, sometimes under the walls of the town, again approaching the camp near the ships. Especially active in support of the Greeks are Hera, Athene, and Poseidon[1] (Neptune) ; and on the side of the Trojans, Aphrodite, Ares, and Apollo.

In the tenth year of the siege, the Greeks sack a neighboring town, and among the captives is Chryseïs,[2] daughter of a priest of Apollo. In the division of spoils, the maid is allotted to Agamemnon, who refuses to restore her to her father when he comes to the camp offering a ransom for her return. The priest, repulsed, prays for vengeance to his god, who sends a plague upon the camp. After nine days, an assembly is called to determine the cause of the pestilence, and Calchas,[3] the seer, declares it to be due to Agamemnon's refusal to restore the daughter of the priest. Finally Agamemnon sends her back, but in anger he takes another maid, Briseïs, from Achilles, to whom the Greeks had given her. Thus arose that anger of Achilles which forms the central idea of the *Iliad* and gives it unity.

Professor Jebb, in his *Introduction to Homer*, gives the following summary of the *Iliad* by books :

I. In the tenth year of the war, Apollo plagues the Greeks, because the daughter of Chryses,[4] his priest, has been taken by

---

[1] Po-sei'-don (-sī'-).
[2] Chrȳ-sē'-is.
[3] Căl'-chas.
[4] Chrȳ-sēṣ.

Agamemnon ; who, being required to restore her, wrongs Achilles by depriving him of his captive, the maiden Briseïs. Thereupon Achilles retires from the war, and Zeus swears to Thetis, the hero's mother, that the Greeks shall rue this wrong done to her son.

II. Zeus sends the Dream-god to the sleeping Agamemnon, and beguiles him to marshal all his host for battle. An assembly of the Greek army shows that the general voice is for going back to Greece ; but at last the army is rallied. — Catalogue of the Greek and Trojan forces (vv. 484–877).

III. The Trojan Paris having challenged the Greek Menelaüs to decide the war by single combat, a truce is made between the armies. Helen and Priam survey the Greek host from the walls of Troy. In the single combat, Aphrodite saves Paris.

IV. The Trojan Pandarus [1] breaks the truce. Agamemnon marshals the Greek host. The armies join battle.

V. The prowess of the Greek Diomede,[2] who makes great slaughter of the Trojans, and, helped by Athene, wounds even Aphrodite and Ares.

VI. Diomede and the Lycian Glaucus (a Trojan ally) are about to fight, when they recognise each other as hereditary guest-friends, and part in amity. — Hector goes from the battle to Troy, and before sallying out again, bids farewell to his wife Andromache.[3]

VII. Single combat of Hector and Ajax. Burying of the dead. The Greeks build a wall to protect their camp by the Helles-pont.[4]

VIII. Zeus, on Olympus, commands the gods to help neither side ; and then, going down to Ida, gives the Trojans the advantage over the Greeks. At Hector's instance the Trojans bivouac on the battle-field.

IX. Agamemnon sends envoys (Odysseus,[5] Ajax, Phœnix) by night to Achilles, offering to restore Briseïs and to make amends ; but Achilles rejects the offer.

[1] Păn'-da-rus.
[2] Dĭ'-o-mēde (*other forms of the same name are* Dĭ'-o-mĕd *and* Dī-o-mē'-dēs).
[3] An-drŏm'-a-chē.
[4] Hĕl'-lĕs-pont.
[5] O-dўs'-seūs.

X. Odysseus and Diomede, going by night towards the Trojan camp, slay Dolon, a Trojan spy ; then they slay the sleeping Rhesus, chief of the Thracians, and take his horses.

XI. Agamemnon does great deeds, but in vain ; many of the leading Greek chiefs are disabled ; and Patroclus,[1] sent by Achilles to ask about the wounded physician Machaon,[2] learns that the plight of the Greeks is desperate.

XII. The Trojans, led by Hector, break through the wall of the Greek camp.

XIII. Zeus having turned his eyes for a while away from the Trojan plain, the sea-god Poseidon, watching from the peak of Samothrace,[3] seizes the moment to encourage the Greeks. The Cretan Idomeneus[4] does great deeds.

XIV. The Sleep-god and Hera lull Zeus to slumber on Mt. Ida. Poseidon urges on the Greeks, and the Trojan Hector is wounded.

XV. Zeus awakens on Mt. Ida. At his bidding, Apollo puts new strength into Hector. The Trojan host presses again on the Greek ships : Ajax valorously defends them.

XVI. Patroclus intercedes for the Greeks with Achilles, who lends him his armour. In the guise of his friend, Patroclus takes the field, and drives the Trojans from the ships ; and at last is slain by Hector.

XVII. The Greeks and Trojans contend for the corpse of Patroclus. Menelaüs does great deeds.

XVIII. Achilles learns the death of Patroclus, and makes moan for him ; at the sound whereof Thetis rises from the sea, and comes to her son. She persuades the god of fire, Hephæstus, to make new armour for Achilles. The shield wrought by Hephæstus is described.

XIX. Achilles renounces his wrath. He is reconciled to Agamemnon before the assembly of the Greek host. He makes ready to go forth to war with them ; the horses are yoked to his chariot ; when the horse Xanthus speaks with human voice, and foretells the doom of Achilles.

[1] Pa-trō'-clus.
[2] Ma-chā'-on.
[3] Sa-mo-thrā'-çē.
[4] I-dŏm'-e-neūs.

XX. The gods come down from Olympus to join in the fight on the Trojan plain — some with the Greeks, some with the Trojans. Achilles fights with Æneas, who is saved by Poseidon ; and with Hector, who is saved by Apollo.

XXI. The river-god Scamander fights with Achilles, who is saved by Hephæstus.

XXII. Achilles fights with Hector, and chases him thrice round the walls of Troy. Zeus weighs in golden scales the lots of Achilles and Hector. Hector is doomed to die : Apollo deserts him, while Athene encourages Achilles. Achilles slays Hector.

XXIII. The spirit of Patroclus appears to Achilles, and craves burial for the corpse : which is burned on a great pyre, with slaying of many victims : twelve Trojan captives are slain, and cast on the pyre. Games follow, in honour of the funeral.

XXIV. As Achilles daily drags the corpse of Hector round the barrow of Patroclus, Apollo pleads with the gods, and Zeus stirs up Priam to go and ransom the body of his son. The god Hermes,[1] in disguise, conducts the aged king across the plain ; Achilles receives him courteously, and accepts the ransom ; and Priam goes back to Troy with the corpse of Hector, to be mourned and buried.

The action of the *Iliad* covers a period of only forty-nine days, of which twenty-one are included in Book I. Books II.–XXII. belong to the next six days. Book XXIII. is devoted to the burial of Patroclus and the funeral games in his honor. In Book XXIV. Achilles abuses Hector's body for twelve days (27th–38th); and the remaining eleven days are taken up with the lament for Hector, his burial, and the erection of a mound over his body. The quarrel of Achilles and Agamemnon occurs on the tenth day, and their reconciliation is effected on the twenty-seventh ; so that the " wrath " lasts seventeen days.

The student who desires to read more about Homer, the poems, the Homeric Age, and kindred subjects, will find

[1] Her'-mēṣ.

Jebb's *Introduction to Homer* perhaps the best single book. The Introduction in Seymour's *School Iliad*, or in Perrin and Seymour's *School Odyssey*, while intended especially for the use of those about to begin the study of the poem in the Greek, is an excellent short exposition for the general reader. Leaf's *Companion to the Iliad* consists primarily of an admirable commentary to be used in connection with a reading of the poem. Mahaffy's *Social Life in Greece* contains two chapters on the Homeric Age. Matthew Arnold's *On Translating Homer* and Professor Wilson's *Homer and His Translators* are valuable contributions to their subjects. The student may also consult Blackie's *Homer and the Iliad*, Lang's *Homer and the Epic*, and Gladstone's various books, the primer on *Homer*, the *Studies on Homer*, and *Juventus Mundi*. Chapters and articles will be found also in any good history of Greece, history of Greek Literature, encyclopedia, or classical dictionary. There are, of course, many other books and articles of varying merit, besides the numerous critical editions and scholia, concordances, and works relating to Homeric antiquities.

The reader should have at hand a good classical atlas and classical dictionary, and should form the habit of looking up the location of places and the accounts of mythological characters. In this connection, Gayley's *Classic Myths in English Literature* will prove helpful to the student of English.

ALEXANDER POPE.

The student who makes the acquaintance of Homer through the medium of Pope's translation, should know something of Pope's personality and environment, the conditions which gave to Pope's *Iliad* a character in many respects quite different from the original.

Alexander Pope, whose father was a London merchant, was born in that city, May 21, 1688, and died at Twickenham, May 30, 1744. From his father he inherited a crooked figure, from his mother a tendency to headache. Thus, all his life, he was unfitted to take part in the vigorous exercises usual to boys and men. Yet he is said to have been a sweet-tempered child, and his pleasant voice caused him to be known among his friends as "the little nightingale." Sweetness of temper, however, can hardly be said to have been a conspicuous trait of Pope, as he revealed himself to the world.

The Popes were Roman Catholics, a fact which had a marked influence on the training of the poet. For in the very year of the latter's birth, James II. fled from England, and an era of greater hardship for Catholics began. The religion of the Pope family, doubtless, was the cause of a large measure of seclusion from the rest of the world, and at the same time closed against the son the entrance to a public career and most positions of honor or authority.

Pope was a precocious boy, whose education, after the age of twelve, consisted almost entirely in reading according to his own whim. His natural taste combined with the family seclusion and his physical deformities to turn his attention to literature ; and, at a very early age, he consciously chose a career in letters, bending every energy of his mind to that calling. The eminent success which he achieved is one of the most conspicuous examples of the triumph of intellect and will over most unfavorable conditions.

At the time of Pope's birth, the conditions which had produced the wonderful works of the imagination that appeared in the reigns of Elizabeth and James I., had completely changed. A new era had come in, which felt the influence of the brilliant French men of letters, who were shedding such lustre on the long reign of Louis XIV. Milton had died fourteen years before Pope was born ; Dryden, at the height of his literary power, had yet twelve years to live ; Swift was a young man of twenty-one, Addison a youth of sixteen, and Steele a boy of thirteen.

Pope's early devotion to literature and his feeling for his master Dryden, are well illustrated by a story which tells of his having prevailed upon an older friend to take him to Will's, that the boy might get a glimpse of the great Dryden surrounded by friends and admirers.

It is said that the young poet was in the habit of submitting his verses to the criticism of his father, who, when not satisfied, would hand them back with the comment, " These are not good rhymes." His model was Dryden, for whom he always retained the greatest admiration, and from whom alone he declared that he had learned versification. The famous advice which he received from Walsh, a critic of the day, well shows the standard of the age. According to Walsh, none of our great poets had been " correct " ; and he, therefore, advised Pope to strive above all things for this quality of "correctness." Certainly, no other quality could have satisfied so fully the taste of that conventional age.

The change which had taken place since the Elizabethan era was very marked. The literature of the earlier period was characterized by a largeness of thought, a splendor of imagery, a wealth and stateliness of language, quite foreign to the more precise spirit of Queen Anne's time. Shakespeare's fancy wandered unchecked, and the poet's language followed the free rein of his fancy. No imagery was too extravagant, if only it had beauty. These peculiarities extended even to the prose of that period. The writers of Pope's time, on the contrary, avoided extremes. They had acquired the ability to express thought concisely and clearly, to say what they wished with precision and force, — qualities so eminently characteristic of the French language. In this, as well as in the method and direction of thought, may be seen the influence of the French writers. Thus we find the writings of Pope's day marked by keen wit, by satire and epigram, by careful attention to correctness of form and as careful avoidance of extremes. The atmosphere is that of the club or the drawing-room, not of the open sky; the music is that of a well-tuned instrument, not of the brook or the lark.

As an indication of Pope's adherence to a standard of form, it is interesting to observe that, besides the translations of the *Iliad* and *Odyssey*, we have 15,851 verses of his, of which 14,383 are in the same metre as the two translations, — namely, the iambic pentameter, or verse of ten syllables and five accents.

Almost from the time that Pope first made the acquaintance of other men of letters to the very end of his life, he was engaged in quarrels, misunderstandings, and controversies. It is clear that he resorted to trickery and falsehood, that he was suspicious and spiteful, and that he was capable of having recourse to unworthy methods in order to enhance his own reputation or to cast aspersion upon an opponent. The acts resulting from these traits gave rise to violent discussions regarding the real character of the man, discussions which have not even yet become settled. But, fortunately, the reader is far more concerned with his character as a poet and his position in literature than with his character as a man and his relation to society.

The seriousness of the youth's ambition appears in the fact that before the age of fifteen he composed an epic on *Alcander, Prince of Rhodes*, in which he sought to emulate the merits of Milton, Spenser, Dryden, Homer, Virgil, Ovid, and others, both ancient and modern.

When about seventeen, he formed the acquaintance of certain men devoted to literature, and through these some of his youthful verses attracted attention. His first published work consisted of *Pastorals*, chiefly notable as exercises by means of which the author was acquiring that perfection of form which was to give him the foremost place among the poets of his time.

The *Essay on Criticism*, published in 1711, shows the same careful correction, and reveals qualities of taste and a mastery of the theory of the art quite remarkable in a man so young. The epigrammatic expression of commonplace truths is a striking feature of the poem.

Pope's progress in the favor of his contemporaries was rapid. Four years after the publication of the *Essay on Criticism*, the first volume of his *Translation of the Iliad* appeared (1715). This work was published in instalments, the sixth and last volume being issued in 1720. The success of the translation was immediate and unquestioned, and established the author as the acknowledged chief among the poets of the day. The story of the financial success is a familiar one, — how Pope received from the sales a sum that enabled him to be comfortable and independent for the rest of his life.

Before the appearance of the *Iliad*, he had published *Windsor Forest*, *Wife of Bath*, *Rape of the Lock*, and a few other poems. In 1717 appeared *Eloisa to Abelard*. Later he published a *Translation of the Odyssey* (less successful than the *Iliad*), and an edition of *Shakespeare*, which did not meet with much favor. Among the more conspicuous of his later writings are the *Dunciad*, the *Moral Essays*, the *Essay on Man*, the *Imitations of Horace*, and the *Epistle to Dr. Arbuthnot*.

As a satirist Pope was brilliant and unsparing, and it was largely his use of this weapon that stirred up those animosities that so embittered his sensitive nature. His cynicism, his fondness for epigram and startling antitheses, his moral standards, and his views of society, were essentially those of the England of his time, — a time when the wit was the most conspicuous figure in society and in letters, when sparkling epigram and neatly turned phrase were more highly esteemed than the loftiest flight of poetic imagination. According to those standards, Pope was the ablest and most skilful poet of his time, and his polished verses may well serve as models of literary form. " From the ranks of English poetry," says a critic, "between the English Revolution and the French, though neither in force nor in fancy nor in pathos was he without superiors, Pope stands prominently forward, the representative of the Muses and the embodiment of English genius."

The most pleasing of his poems, in the opinion of a great majority of readers, is the *Rape of the Lock*, a mock heroic based upon the theft of a lock of hair from a Miss Fermor by a certain young lord, and written with a view of removing the unpleasant feeling between the two families which had resulted from that episode. The best specimens of Pope's satire are perhaps to be found in the famous portraits of Addison, Halifax, the Duchess of Marlborough, and others, contained in the *Imitations of Horace*. Probably the performance by which he has been best known outside of England, is the *Essay on Man*, a professed philosophical treatise in verse. The *Dunciad*, in which he holds up to ridicule, under the guise of dunce, nearly every man of his time who had incurred his displeasure, is keen and brilliant, and contains some of the most perfect specimens of his art; but most of its allusions would be unintelligible to the general reader of our day. His name, for English readers at least, has come to be associated especially with his translations of the *Iliad* and the *Odyssey*, particularly the former.

Those who are desirous of obtaining further information regarding Pope's life and period will find a good summary in Allibone's *Dictionary of English Literature.* Leslie Stephen's *Life of Pope* and the biography by Samuel Johnson are among the best. A comprehensive *Life* is that by Carruthers; while the student may consult also the biographies by Dyce, Ward, Chalmers, and Anderson, as well as the very full introductions in Elwin's edition. Disraeli's *Quarrels of Authors*, Jameson's *Loves of the Poets*, Howitt's *Homes and Haunts of the British Poets*, Cobbett's *Memorials of Twickenham*, will prove helpful. Lowell's essay in *My Study Windows* is recommended ; and the student will have no difficulty in finding an abundance of articles in the best periodicals. Thackeray and Macaulay both have written much about the period in different essays. Of course, the standard histories contain accounts of the life and events of that time.

POPE'S HOMER : OTHER TRANSLATIONS OF THE ILIAD.

In reading Pope's *Iliad*, it is important to keep in mind that much of it is Pope and not Homer. It would hardly be possible for any one not familiar with Homer in the Greek to appreciate closely the differences between the two ; but the student who has come to know the general characteristics of Homer and of Pope will not fail to recognize in the translation many passages which reflect only the thoughts and feelings and taste of the translator.

Probably what has already been said of Homer and of Pope may serve to indicate or suggest the vast differences between the two. It should not be forgotten that Homer, as Matthew Arnold expresses it, is "rapid in his movement, plain in his words and style, simple in his ideas, noble in his manner." No translation has approached the original in excellence.

Yet it would be a serious blunder to conclude that Pope's *Iliad* has not strong claims to a high place in our English

literature.   There have been many translations of Homer,
both in verse and prose; but probably no other in our language has been so widely read and so commonly admired.
Pope, in his Preface, says:

   . . . It is not to be doubted that the *fire* of the poem is what a
translator should principally regard, as it is most likely to expire
in his managing. . . .   Upon the whole, I must confess myself
utterly incapable of doing justice to Homer.   I attempt him in no
other hope but that which one may entertain without much vanity,
of giving a more tolerable copy of him than any entire translation
in verse has yet done. . . .   That which in my opinion ought to
be the endeavour of any one who translates Homer, is above all
things to keep alive that spirit and fire which makes his chief
character: in particular places, where the sense can bear any
doubt, to follow the strongest and most poetical, as most agreeing
with that character ; to copy him in all the variations of his style,
and the different modulations of his numbers ; to preserve, in the
more active or descriptive parts, a warmth and elevation; in the
more sedate or narrative, a plainness and solemnity; in the speeches,
a fullness and perspicuity ; in the sentences, a shortness and grav-
ity ; not to neglect even the little figures and turns on the words,
nor sometimes the very cast of the periods ; neither to omit nor
confound any rites or customs of antiquity.

   It will be interesting for the reader to observe to what
extent Pope has followed the principles which he here lays
down.   It will be interesting, also, to compare his translation
with others.   The non-classical student will, of course, find
it impossible to make the comparison with the original ; but
for the English student the prose version by Lang, Leaf,
and Myers may serve to express accurately the sense, in
language suggesting the simplicity and dignity of the Greek.
   Only one passage will be selected here for such comparison as has been suggested, — the famous simile at the close of
Book VIII.   The conflict near the ships, which has proved

so nearly fatal to the Greeks, has been interrupted by the
approach of night ; and the Trojans have encamped on the
plain to await the coming of day, that they may renew
the contest. Homer then, in the last thirteen lines of the
book, gives a characteristic description of the host.

Mr. Walter Leaf, in the admirable prose version already
referred to, renders the passage thus :

But these with high hopes sate them all night along the high-
ways of the battle, and their watchfires burned in multitude.
Even as when in heaven the stars about the bright moon shine
clear to see, when the air is windless, and all the peaks appear
and the tall headlands and glades, and from heaven breaketh open
the infinite air, and all stars are seen, and the shepherd's heart is
glad ; even in like multitude between the ships and the streams of
Xanthos appeared the watchfires that the Trojans kindled in front
of Ilios. A thousand fires burned in the plain and by the side of
each sate fifty in the gleam of blazing fire. And the horses
champed white barley and spelt, and standing by their chariots
waited for the throned Dawn.

Chapman (1557–1634) :

And spent all night in open fields; fires round about them shined,
As when about the silver moone, when aire is free from winde,
The stars shine clear, to whose sweet beams high prospects and
      the brows
Of all steepe hills and pinnacles thrust up themselves for showes ;
And even the lowly vallies joy, to glitter in their sight,
When the unmeasured firmament bursts to disclose her light,
And all the signes in heaven are seen, that glad the shepherd's
      heart :
So many fires disclosed their beames, made by the Trojan part,
Before the face of Ilion ; and her bright turrets show'd.
A thousand courts of guard kept fires ; and every guard allow'd
Fiftie stout men, by whom their horse eate oates and hard white
      corne,
And all did wilfully expect the silver-throned morne.

Ogilby (1600–1676) :

All night in field insulting Trojans lie,
And towring smoak ascends the gloomy skie.
So glorious stars about the moon are seen,
When winds are silent and the air serene ;
Steep mountain-clifts, vallies and towers appear,
And star-bestudded skies expansions clear :
The swain rejoyceth viewing then the stars,
And elements at truce from civil wars.
So many fires clear'd up the Trojan ranks
Betwixt the navie and Scamander's banks.
A thousand flames made bright the Dardan camps:
Fifty at each sate free from chilling damps.
Their horses feed on oats and purest corn,
Ty'd to their chariots, and expect the morn.

Pope (1688–1744):

The troops exulting sate in order round,
And beaming fires illumin'd all the ground,
As when the moon, refulgent lamp of night !
O'er heav'n's clear azure spreads her sacred light,
When not a breath disturbs the deep serene,
And not a cloud o'ercasts the solemn scene ;
Around her throne the vivid planets roll,
And stars unnumber'd gild the glowing pole,
O'er the dark trees a yellower verdure shed,
And tip with silver ev'ry mountain's head ;
Then shine the vales, the rocks in prospect rise,
A flood of glory bursts from all the skies :
The conscious swains, rejoicing in the sight,
Eye the blue vault, and bless the useful light.
So many flames before proud Ilion blaze,
And lighten glimm'ring Xanthus with their rays :
The long reflections of the distant fires
Gleam on the walls, and tremble on the spires.
A thousand piles the dusky horrours gild,

And shoot a shady lustre o'er the field.
Full fifty guards each flaming pile attend,
Whose umber'd arms by fits thick flashes send ;
Loud neigh the coursers o'er their heaps of corn,
And ardent warriors wait the rising morn.

   Cowper (1731–1800):

Big with great purposes and proud, they sat,
Not disarray'd, but in fair form disposed
Of even ranks, and watch'd their numerous fires,
As when around the clear bright moon, the stars
Shine in full splendour, and the winds are hush'd,
The groves, the mountain-tops, the headland heights,
Stand all apparent, not a vapour streaks
The boundless blue and ether open'd wide ;
All glitters, and the shepherd's heart is cheer'd.
So numerous seem'd those fires, between the stream
Of Xanthus blazing, and the fleet of Greece,
In prospect all of Troy, a thousand fires,
Each watch'd by fifty warriors, seated near ;
The steeds beside the chariot stood, their corn
Chewing, and waiting till the golden-throned
Aurora should restore the light of day.

   Sotheby (1757–1833) :

But Troy elate, in orderly array,
All night around her numerous watch-fires lay, —
As when in heaven the stars at night's still noon,
Beam in their brightness round the full-orb'd moon,
When sleeps the wind, and every mountain height,
Rocks, cliffs, and groves, shine towering up in light,
And the vast firmament immensely riven,
Expands for other stars another heaven,
Gladd'ning the shepherd's heart ; so numerous rose
The watch-fires round the warriors' arm'd repose,
In sight of Troy, and wide illumed the scene

The flow of Xanthus and the fleet between :
A thousand fires : and each with separate blaze
O'er fifty warriors cast the undying rays,
Where, ranged beside the cars, full-fed with corn,
The steeds impatient stood, and snuff'd the coming morn.

Edward, Earl of Derby (1799–1869):

Full of proud hopes, upon the pass of war,
All night they camped ; and frequent blazed their fires.
As when in Heaven, around the glittering moon
The stars shine bright amid the breathless air ;
And every crag, and every jutting peak
Stands boldly forth, and every forest glade ;
Even to the gates of Heaven is opened wide
The boundless sky ; shines each particular star
Distinct ; joy fills the gazing shepherd's heart.
So bright, so thickly scattered o'er the plain,
Before the walls of Troy, between the ships
And Xanthus' stream, the Trojan watchfires blazed.
A thousand burnt brightly ; and round each
Sat fifty warriors in the ruddy glare ;
Champing the provender before them laid,
Barley and rye, the tethered horses stood
Beside the cars, and waited for the morn.

Bryant (1794–1878):

So, high in hope, they sat the whole night through
In warlike lines, and many watch-fires blazed.
As when in heaven the stars look brightly forth
Round the clear-shining moon, while not a breeze
Stirs in the depths of air, and all the stars
Are seen, and gladness fills the shepherd's heart,
So many fires in sight of Ilium blazed,
Lit by the sons of Troy, between the ships
And eddying Xanthus : on the plain there shone
A thousand ; fifty warriors by each fire

Sat in its light.   Their steeds beside the cars —
Champing their oats and their white barley — stood,
And waited for the golden morn to rise.

Tennyson translates the passage :

As when in heaven the stars about the moon
Look beautiful, when all the winds are laid,
And every height comes out, and jutting peak
And valley, and the immeasurable heavens
Break open to their highest, and all the stars
Shine, and the shepherd gladdens in his heart :
So many a fire between the ships and stream
Of Xanthus blazed before the towers of Troy,
A thousand on the plain ; and close by each
Sat fifty in the blaze of burning fire ;
And champing golden grain, the horses stood
Hard by their chariots, waiting for the dawn.

Matthew Arnold translates the last verses :

So shone forth, in front of Troy, by the bed of the Xanthus,
Between that and the ships, the Trojans' numerous fires.
In the plain there were kindled a thousand fires : by each one
There sat fifty men in the ruddy light of the fire :
By their chariots stood the steeds and champed the white barley
While their masters sat by the fire and waited for morning.

POPE'S ILIAD

From a "Tabula Iliaca." Relief in Berlin Antiquarium. The figure of the
old man reading is supposed to represent Homer.

POPE'S ILIAD.

BOOK I.

THE CONTENTION OF
ACHILLES AND AGAMEMNON.

ACHILLES' wrath, to Greece the direful spring
Of woes unnumber'd, heav'nly goddess, sing!
That wrath which hurl'd to Pluto's gloomy reign
The souls of mighty chiefs untimely slain;
Whose limbs, unburied on the naked shore,   5
Devouring dogs and hungry vultures tore:
Since great Achilles and Atrides strove,
Such was the sov'reign doom, and such the will of Jove!
    Declare, O Muse! in what ill-fated hour
Sprung the fierce strife, from what offended pow'r?   10
Latona's son a dire contagion spread,
And heap'd the camp with mountains of the dead;
The king of men his rev'rend priest defied,
And, for the king's offence, the people died.
    For Chryses sought with costly gifts to gain   15
His captive daughter from the victor's chain.
Suppliant the venerable father stands;
Apollo's awful ensigns grace his hands:
By these he begs; and, lowly bending down,
Extends the sceptre and the laurel crown.   20

He su'd to all, but chief implor'd for grace
The brother-kings of Atreus' royal race:
"Ye kings and warriors! may your vows be crown'd,
And Troy's proud walls lie level with the ground.
May Jove restore you, when your toils are o'er,　　　25
Safe to the pleasures of your native shore.
But oh! relieve a wretched parent's pain,
And give Chryseïs to these arms again;
If mercy fail, yet let my presents move,
And dread avenging Phœbus, son of Jove."　　　30
　　The Greeks in shouts their joint assent declare,
The priest to rev'rence, and release the fair.
Not so Atrides: he, with kingly pride,
Repuls'd the sacred sire, and thus replied:
"Hence on thy life, and fly these hostile plains,　　　35
Nor ask, presumptuous, what the king detains;
Hence, with thy laurel crown and golden rod,
Nor trust too far those ensigns of thy god.
Mine is thy daughter, priest, and shall remain;
And pray'rs, and tears, and bribes, shall plead in vain;　　40
Till time shall rifle ev'ry youthful grace,
And age dismiss her from my cold embrace,
In daily labours of the loom employ'd,
Or doom'd to deck the bed she once enjoy'd.
Hence then; to Argos shall the maid retire,　　　45
Far from her native soil and weeping sire."
　　The trembling priest along the shore return'd,
And in the anguish of a father mourn'd.
Disconsolate, not daring to complain,
Silent he wander'd by the sounding main;　　　50
Till, safe at distance, to his god he prays,
The god who darts around the world his rays:
"O Smintheus! sprung from fair Latona's line,
Thou guardian pow'r of Cilla the divine,

Thou source of light! whom Tenedos adores,   55
And whose bright presence gilds thy Chrysa's shores;
If e'er with wreaths I hung thy sacred fane,
Or fed the flames with fat of oxen slain;
God of the silver bow! thy shafts employ,
Avenge thy servant, and the Greeks destroy."   60
     Thus Chryses pray'd: the fav'ring pow'r attends,
And from Olympus' lofty tops descends.
Bent was his bow, the Grecian hearts to wound;
Fierce as he mov'd, his silver shafts resound.
Breathing revenge, a sudden night he spread,   65
And gloomy darkness roll'd around his head.
The fleet in view, he twang'd his deadly bow,
And hissing fly the feather'd fates below.
On mules and dogs th' infection first began;
And last, the vengeful arrows fix'd in man.   70
For nine long nights, thro' all the dusky air
The pyres thick-flaming shot a dismal glare.
But ere the tenth revolving day was run,
Inspir'd by Juno, Thetis' god-like son
Conven'd to council all the Grecian train;   75
For much the goddess mourn'd her heroes slain.
     Th' assembly seated, rising o'er the rest,
Achilles thus the king of men address'd:
     "Why leave we not the fatal Trojan shore,
And measure back the seas we cross'd before?   80
The plague destroying whom the sword would spare,
'T is time to save the few remains of war.
But–let some prophet or some sacred sage
Explore the cause of great Apollo's rage;
Or learn the wasteful vengeance to remove   85
By mystic dreams, for dreams descend from Jove.
If broken vows this heavy curse have laid,
Let altars smoke, and hecatombs be paid.

So heav'n aton'd shall dying Greece restore,
And Phœbus dart his burning shafts no more."   90
    He said, and sate : when Calchas thus replied,
Calchas the wise, the Grecian priest and guide,
That sacred seer, whose comprehensive view
The past, the present, and the future knew ;
Uprising slow the venerable sage   95
Thus spoke the prudence and the fears of age :
    "Belov'd of Jove, Achilles! would'st thou know
Why angry Phœbus bends his fatal bow?
First give thy faith, and plight a prince's word
Of sure protection, by thy pow'r and sword.   100
For I must speak what wisdom would conceal,
And truths invidious to the great reveal.
Bold is the task, when subjects, grown too wise,
Instruct a monarch where his error lies ;
For tho' we deem the short-liv'd fury past,   105
'T is sure the mighty will revenge at last."
    To whom Pelides : " From thy inmost soul
Speak what thou know'st, and speak without control.
Ev'n by that god I swear, who rules the day,
To whom thy hands the vows of Greece convey,   110
And whose blest oracles thy lips declare ;
Long as Achilles breathes this vital air,
No daring Greek, of all the num'rous band,
Against his priest shall lift an impious hand :
Not ev'n the chief by whom our hosts are led,   115
The king of kings, shall touch that sacred head."
    Encourag'd thus, the blameless man replies:
" Nor vows unpaid, nor slighted sacrifice,
But he, our chief, provok'd the raging pest,
Apollo's vengeance for his injur'd priest.   120
Nor will the god's awaken'd fury cease,
But plagues shall spread, and fun'ral fires increase,

Till the great king, without a ransom paid,
To her own Chrysa send the black-ey'd maid.
Perhaps, with added sacrifice and pray'r,   125
The priest may pardon, and the god may spare."
   The prophet spoke ; when, with a gloomy frown,
The monarch started from his shining throne ;
Black choler fill'd his breast that boil'd with ire,
And from his eyeballs flash'd the living fire.   130
"Augur accurs'd ! denouncing mischief still,
Prophet of plagues for ever boding ill !
Still must that tongue some wounding message bring,
And still thy priestly pride provoke thy king?
For this are Phœbus' oracles explor'd,   135
To teach the Greeks to murmur at their lord?
For this with falsehoods is my honour stain'd,
Is heav'n offended, and a priest profan'd,
Because my prize, my beauteous maid, I hold,
And heav'nly charms prefer to proffer'd gold?   140
A maid, unmatch'd in manners as in face,
Skill'd in each art, and crown'd with every grace :
Not half so dear were Clytæmnestra's charms,
When first her blooming beauties bless'd my arms.
Yet, if the gods demand her, let her sail ;   145
Our cares are only for the public weal :
Let me be deem'd the hateful cause of all,
And suffer, rather than my people fall.
The prize, the beauteous prize, I will resign,
So dearly valu'd, and so justly mine.   150
But since for common good I yield the fair,
My private loss let grateful Greece repair ;
Nor unrewarded let your prince complain,
That he alone has fought and bled in vain."
   "Insatiate king !" (Achilles thus replies)   155
"Fond of the pow'r, but fonder of the prize !

Would'st thou the Greeks their lawful prey should yield,
The due reward of many a well-fought field?
The spoils of cities raz'd and warriors slain,
We share with justice, as with toil we gain: 160
But to resume whate'er thy av'rice craves
(That trick of tyrants) may be borne by slaves.
Yet if our chief for plunder only fight,
The spoils of Ilion shall thy loss requite,
Whene'er, by Jove's decree, our conqu'ring pow'rs   165
Shall humble to the dust her lofty tow'rs."
    Then thus the king: "Shall I my prize resign
With tame content, and thou possess'd of thine?
Great as thou art, and like a god in fight,
Think not to rob me of a soldier's right.   170
At thy demand shall I restore the maid?
First let the just equivalent be paid;
Such as a king might ask; and let it be
A treasure worthy her, and worthy me.
Or grant me this, or with a monarch's claim   175
This hand shall seize some other captive dame.
The mighty Ajax shall his prize resign,
Ulysses' spoils, or ev'n thy own be mine.
The man who suffers, loudly may complain;
And rage he may, but he shall rage in vain.   180
But this when time requires — it now remains
We launch a bark to plough the wat'ry plains,
And waft the sacrifice to Chrysa's shores,
With chosen pilots, and with lab'ring oars.
Soon shall the fair the sable ship ascend,   185
And some deputed prince the charge attend.
This Creta's king, or Ajax shall fulfil,
Or wise Ulysses see perform'd our will;
Or, if our royal pleasure shall ordain,
Achilles' self conduct her o'er the main;   190

Let fierce Achilles, dreadful in his rage,
The god propitiate, and the pest assuage."
 At this, Pelides, frowning stern, replied:
" O tyrant, arm'd with insolence and pride !
Inglorious slave to int'rest, ever join'd   195
With fraud, unworthy of a royal mind!
What gen'rous Greek, obedient to thy word,
Shall form an ambush, or shall lift the sword?
What cause have I to war at thy decree?
The distant Trojans never injur'd me: 200
To Phthia's realms no hostile troops they led ;
Safe in her vales my warlike coursers fed ;
Far hence remov'd, the hoarse-resounding main
And walls of rocks secure my native reign,
Whose fruitful soil luxuriant harvests grace,   205
Rich in her fruits, and in her martial race.
Hither we sail'd, a voluntary throng,
T' avenge a private, not a public wrong:
What else to Troy th' assembled nations draws,
But thine, ungrateful, and thy brother's cause?   210
Is this the pay our blood and toils deserve,
Disgrac'd and injur'd by the man we serve?
And dar'st thou threat to snatch my prize away,
Due to the deeds of many a dreadful day?
A prize as small, O tyrant ! match'd with thine,   215
As thy own actions if compar'd to mine.
Thine in each conquest is the wealthy prey,
Tho' mine the sweat and danger of the day.
Some trivial present to my ships I bear,
Or barren praises pay the wounds of war.   220
But know, proud monarch, I 'm thy slave no more ;
My fleet shall waft me to Thessalia's shore.
Left by Achilles on the Trojan plain,
What spoils, what conquests, shall Atrides gain ? "

To this the king : " Fly, mighty warrior! fly,   225
Thy aid we need not, and thy threats defy.
There want not chiefs in such a cause to fight,
And Jove himself shall guard a monarch's right.
Of all the kings (the gods' distinguish'd care)
To pow'r superior none such hatred bear :   230
Strife and debate thy restless soul employ,
And wars and horrours are thy savage joy.
If thou hast strength, 't was heav'n that strength bestow'd,
For know, vain man! thy valour is from God.
Haste, launch thy vessels, fly with speed away,   235
Rule thy own realms with arbitrary sway :
I heed thee not, but prize at equal rate
Thy short-liv'd friendship and thy groundless hate.
Go, threat thy earth-born Myrmidons ; but here
'T is mine to threaten, prince, and thine to fear.   240
Know, if the god the beauteous dame demand,
My bark shall waft her to her native land ;
But then prepare, imperious prince! prepare,
Fierce as thou art, to yield thy captive fair :
Ev'n in thy tent I 'll seize the blooming prize,   245
Thy lov'd Briseïs with the radiant eyes.
Hence shalt thou prove my might, and curse the hour,
Thou stood'st a rival of imperial pow'r ;
And hence to all our host it shall be known
That kings are subject to the gods alone."   250
  Achilles heard, with grief and rage oppress'd ;
His heart swell'd high, and labour'd in his breast.
Distracting thoughts by turns his bosom rul'd,
Now fir'd by wrath, and now by reason cool'd :
That prompts his hand to draw the deadly sword,   255
Force thro' the Greeks, and pierce their haughty lord ;
This whispers soft, his vengeance to control,
And calm the rising tempest of his soul.

Just as in anguish of suspense he stay'd,
While half unsheath'd appear'd the glitt'ring blade,   260
Minerva swift descended from above,
Sent by the sister and the wife of Jove
(For both the princes claim'd her equal care);
Behind she stood, and by the golden hair
Achilles seiz'd; to him alone confess'd;   265
A sable cloud conceal'd her from the rest.
He sees, and sudden to the goddess cries
(Known by the flames that sparkle from her eyes):
    " Descends Minerva, in her guardian care,
A heav'nly witness of the wrongs I bear   270
From Atreus' son?   Then let those eyes that view
The daring crime, behold the vengeance too."
    " Forbear!" (the progeny of Jove replies)
" To calm thy fury I forsake the skies:
Let great Achilles, to the gods resign'd,   275
To reason yield the empire o'er his mind.
By awful Juno this command is giv'n;
The king and you are both the care of heav'n.
The force of keen reproaches let him feel,
But sheath, obedient, thy revenging steel.   280
For I pronounce (and trust a heav'nly pow'r)
Thy injur'd honour has its fated hour,
When the proud monarch shall thy arms implore,
And bribe thy friendship with a boundless store.
Then let revenge no longer bear the sway,   285
Command thy passions, and the gods obey."
    To her Pelides: " With regardful ear,
'T is just, O goddess! I thy dictates hear.
Hard as it is, my vengeance I suppress:
Those who revere the gods, the gods will bless."   290
He said, observant of the blue-ey'd maid;
Then in the sheath return'd the shining blade.

The goddess swift to high Olympus flies,
And joins the sacred senate of the skies.

Nor yet the rage his boiling breast forsook,   295
Which thus redoubling on Atrides broke:
"O monster! mix'd of insolence and fear,
Thou dog in forehead, but in heart a deer!
When wert thou known in ambush'd fights to dare,
Or nobly face the horrid front of war?   300
'T is ours, the chance of fighting fields to try,
Thine to look on, and bid the valiant die.
So much 't is safer thro' the camp to go,
And rob a subject, than despoil a foe.
Scourge of thy people, violent and base!   305
Sent in Jove's anger on a slavish race,
Who, lost to sense of gen'rous freedom past,
Are tam'd to wrongs, or this had been thy last.
Now by this sacred sceptre hear me swear,
Which never more shall leaves or blossoms bear,   310
Which, sever'd from the trunk (as I from thee),
On the bare mountains left its parent tree;
This sceptre, form'd by temper'd steel to prove
An ensign of the delegates of Jove,
From whom the pow'r of laws and justice springs   315
(Tremendous oath! inviolate to kings):
By this I swear, when bleeding Greece again
Shall call Achilles, she shall call in vain.
When, flushed with slaughter, Hector comes to spread
The purpled shore with mountains of the dead,   320
Then shalt thou mourn th' affront thy madness gave,
Forc'd to deplore, when impotent to save:
Then rage in bitterness of soul, to know
This act has made the bravest Greek thy foe."

He spoke; and furious hurl'd against the ground   325
His sceptre starr'd with golden studs around;

Then sternly silent sate.   With like disdain,
The raging king return'd his frowns again.
   To calm their passion with the words of age,
Slow from his seat arose the Pylian sage,   330
Experienc'd Nestor, in persuasion skill'd ;
Words sweet as honey from his lips distill'd :
Two generations now had pass'd away,
Wise by his rules, and happy by his sway ;
Two ages o'er his native realm he reign'd,   335
And now th' example of the third remain'd.
All view'd with awe the venerable man ;
Who thus, with mild benevolence, began :
   "What shame, what woe is this to Greece ! what joy
To Troy's proud monarch and the friends of Troy !   340
That adverse gods commit to stern debate
The best, the bravest of the Grecian state.
Young as ye are, this youthful heat restrain,
Nor think your Nestor's years and wisdom vain.
A godlike race of heroes once I knew,   345
Such as no more these aged eyes shall view !
Lives there a chief to match Pirithous' fame,
Dryas the bold, or Ceneus' deathless name ;
Theseus, endu'd with more than mortal might,
Or Polyphemus, like the gods in fight ?   350
With these of old to toils of battle bred,
In early youth my hardy days I led ;
Fir'd with the thirst which virtuous envy breeds,
And smit with love of honourable deeds.
Strongest of men, they pierc'd the mountain boar,   355
Rang'd the wild deserts red with monsters' gore,
And from their hills the shaggy Centaurs tore.
Yet these with soft persuasive arts I sway'd ;
When Nestor spoke, they listen'd and obey'd.
If in my youth, ev'n these esteem'd me wise,   360

Do you, young warriors, hear my age advise.
Atrides, seize not on the beauteous slave;
That prize the Greeks by common suffrage gave:
Nor thou, Achilles, treat our prince with pride;
Let kings be just, and sov'reign pow'r preside.   365
Thee the first honours of the war adorn,
Like gods in strength, and of a goddess born;
Him awful majesty exalts above
The pow'rs of earth and sceptred sons of Jove.
Let both unite with well-consenting mind,   370
So shall authority with strength be join'd.
Leave me, O king! to calm Achilles' rage;
Rule thou thyself, as more advanc'd in age.
Forbid it, gods! Achilles should be lost,
The pride of Greece, and bulwark of our host."   375
    This said, he ceas'd; the king of men replies:
"Thy years are awful, and thy words are wise.
But that imperious, that unconquer'd soul,
No laws can limit, no respect control:
Before his pride must his superiors fall,   380
His word the law, and he the lord of all?
Him must our hosts, our chiefs, ourself obey?
What king can bear a rival in his sway?
Grant that the gods his matchless force have giv'n;
Has foul reproach a privilege from heav'n?"   385
    Here on the monarch's speech Achilles broke,
And furious, thus, and interrupting, spoke:
"Tyrant, I well deserv'd thy galling chain,
To live thy slave, and still to serve in vain,
Should I submit to each unjust decree: 390
Command thy vassals, but command not me.
Seize on Briseïs, whom the Grecians doom'd
My prize of war, yet tamely see resum'd;
And seize secure; no more Achilles draws

His conqu'ring sword in any woman's cause.   395
The gods command me to forgive the past ;
But let this first invasion be the last :
For know, thy blood, when next thou dar'st invade,
Shall stream in vengeance on my reeking blade."
    At this they ceas'd ; the stern debate expir'd :   400
The chiefs in sullen majesty retir'd.
    Achilles with Patroclus took his way,
Where near his tents his hollow vessels lay.
Meantime Atrides launch'd with num'rous oars
A well-rigg'd ship for Chrysa's sacred shores :   405
High on the deck was fair Chryseïs plac'd,
And sage Ulysses with the conduct grac'd :
Safe in her sides the hecatomb they stow'd,
Then, swiftly sailing, cut the liquid road.
    The host to expiate, next the king prepares,   410
With pure lustrations and with solemn pray'rs.
Wash'd by the briny wave, the pious train
Are cleans'd ; and cast th' ablutions in the main.
Along the shores whole hecatombs were laid,
And bulls and goats to Phœbus' altars paid.   415
The sable fumes in curling spires arise,
And waft their grateful odours to the skies.
    The army thus in sacred rites engag'd,
Atrides still with deep resentment rag'd.
To wait his will two sacred heralds stood,   420
Talthybius and Eurybates the good.
" Haste to the fierce Achilles' tent," he cries,
" Thence bear Briseïs as our royal prize :
Submit he must ; or, if they will not part,
Ourself in arms shall tear her from his heart."   425
    Th' unwilling heralds act their lord's commands ;
Pensive they walk along the barren sands :
Arriv'd, the hero in his tent they find,

With gloomy aspect, on his arm reclin'd.
At awful distance long they silent stand,   430
Loth to advance or speak their hard command ;
Decent confusion !   This the godlike man
Perceiv'd, and thus with accent mild began :
    "With leave and honour enter our abodes,
Ye sacred ministers of men and gods !   435
I know your message ; by constraint you came ;
Not you, but your imperious lord, I blame.
Patroclus, haste, the fair Briseïs bring ;
Conduct my captive to the haughty king.
But witness, heralds, and proclaim my vow,   440
Witness to gods above and men below !
But first and loudest to your prince declare,
That lawless tyrant whose commands you bear ;
Unmov'd as death Achilles shall remain,
Tho' prostrate Greece should bleed at ev'ry vein :   445
The raging chief in frantic passion lost,
Blind to himself, and useless to his host,
Unskill'd to judge the future by the past,
In blood and slaughter shall repent at last."
    Patroclus now th' unwilling beauty brought ;   450
She, in soft sorrows and in pensive thought,
Pass'd silent, as the heralds held her hand,
And oft look'd back, slow-moving o'er the strand.
    Not so his loss the fierce Achilles bore ;
But sad retiring to the sounding shore,   455
O'er the wild margin of the deep he hung,
That kindred deep from whence his mother sprung ;
There, bath'd in tears of anger and disdain,
Thus loud lamented to the stormy main :
    "O parent goddess ! since in early bloom   460
Thy son must fall, by too severe a doom ;
Sure, to so short a race of glory born,

Great Jove in justice should this span adorn.
Honour and fame at least the Thund'rer ow'd;
And ill he pays the promise of a god,   465
If yon proud monarch thus thy son defies,
Obscures my glories, and resumes my prize."
　　Far in the deep recesses of the main,
Where aged Ocean holds his wat'ry reign,
The goddess-mother heard.　The waves divide;   470
And like a mist she rose above the tide;
Beheld him mourning on the naked shores,
And thus the sorrows of his soul explores:
" Why grieves my son? Thy anguish let me share,
Reveal the cause, and trust a parent's care."   475
　　He deeply sighing said: " To tell my woe
Is but to mention what too well you know.
From Thebe, sacred to Apollo's name,
Eëtion's realm, our conqu'ring army came,
With treasure loaded and triumphant spoils,   480
Whose just division crown'd the soldier's toils;
But bright Chryseïs, heav'nly prize! was led
By vote selected to the gen'ral's bed.
The priest of Phœbus sought by gifts to gain
His beauteous daughter from the victor's chain;   485
The fleet he reach'd, and, lowly bending down,
Held forth the sceptre and the laurel crown,
Entreating all; but chief implor'd for grace
The brother-kings of Atreus' royal race:
The gen'rous Greeks their joint consent declare,   490
The priest to rev'rence, and release the fair.
Not so Atrides: he, with wonted pride,
The sire insulted, and his gifts denied:
Th' insulted sire (his god's peculiar care)
To Phœbus pray'd, and Phœbus heard the pray'r: 495
A dreadful plague ensues; th' avenging darts

Incessant fly, and pierce the Grecian hearts.
A prophet then, inspir'd by heav'n, arose,
And points the crime, and thence derives the woes:
Myself the first th' assembled chiefs incline   500
T' avert the vengeance of the pow'r divine;
Then, rising in his wrath, the monarch storm'd;
Incens'd he threaten'd, and his threats perform'd:
The fair Chryseïs to her sire was sent,
With offer'd gifts to make the god relent;   505
But now he seiz'd Briseïs' heav'nly charms,
And of my valour's prize defrauds my arms,
Defrauds the votes of all the Grecian train;
And service, faith, and justice plead in vain.
But, goddess! thou thy suppliant son attend,   510
To high Olympus' shining court ascend,
Urge all the ties to former service ow'd,
And sue for vengeance to the thund'ring god.
Oft hast thou triumph'd in the glorious boast
That thou stood'st forth, of all the æthereal host,   515
When bold rebellion shook the realms above,
Th' undaunted guard of cloud-compelling Jove;
When the bright partner of his awful reign,
The warlike maid, and monarch of the main,
The traitor-gods, by mad ambition driv'n,   520
Durst threat with chains th' omnipotence of heav'n.
Then call'd by thee, the monster Titan came
(Whom gods Briareüs, men Ægeon name);
Thro' wond'ring skies enormous stalk'd along;
Not he that shakes the solid earth so strong: 525
With giant-pride at Jove's high throne he stands,
And brandish'd round him all his hundred hands.
Th' affrighted gods confess'd their awful lord,
They dropp'd the fetters, trembled and ador'd.
This, goddess, this to his rememb'rance call,   530

Embrace his knees, at his tribunal fall ;
Conjure him far to drive the Grecian train,
To hurl them headlong to their fleet and main,
To heap the shores with copious death, and bring
The Greeks to know the curse of such a king :			535
Let Agamemnon lift his haughty head
O'er all his wide dominion of the dead,
And mourn in blood, that e'er he durst disgrace
The boldest warrior of the Grecian race."

"Unhappy son !" (fair Thetis thus replies,			540
While tears celestial trickle from her eyes)
"Why have I borne thee with a mother's throes,
To fates averse, and nurs'd for future woes ?
So short a space the light of heav'n to view !
So short a space ! and fill'd with sorrow, too !			545
Oh, might a parent's careful wish prevail,
Far, far from Ilion should thy vessels sail,
And thou, from camps remote, the danger shun,
Which now, alas ! too nearly threats my son.
Yet (what I can) to move thy suit I 'll go			550
To great Olympus crown'd with fleecy snow.
Meantime, secure within thy ships, from far
Behold the field, nor mingle in the war.
The sire of gods, and all th' æthereal train,
On the warm limits of the farthest main,			555
Now mix with mortals, nor disdain to grace
The feasts of Æthiopia's blameless race :
Twelve days the pow'rs indulge the genial rite,
Returning with the twelfth revolving light.
Then will I mount the brazen dome, and move			560
The high tribunal of immortal Jove."

The goddess spoke : the rolling waves unclose ;
Then down the deep she plung'd, from whence she
		rose,

And left him sorrowing on the lonely coast,
In wild resentment for the fair he lost.   565
    In Chrysa's port now sage Ulysses rode;
Beneath the deck the destin'd victims stow'd:
The sails they furl'd, they lash'd the mast aside,
And dropp'd their anchors, and the pinnace tied.
Next on the shore their hecatomb they land,   570
Chryseïs last descending on the strand.
Her, thus returning from the furrow'd main,
Ulysses led to Phœbus' sacred fane;
Where, at his solemn altar, as the maid
He gave to Chryses, thus the hero said: 575
    "Hail, rev'rend priest! to Phœbus' awful dome
A suppliant I from great Atrides come:
Unransom'd here receive the spotless fair;
Accept the hecatomb the Greeks prepare;
And may thy god, who scatters darts around,   580
Aton'd by sacrifice, desist to wound."
    At this the sire embrac'd the maid again,
So sadly lost, so lately sought in vain.
Then near the altar of the darting king,
Dispos'd in rank their hecatomb they bring: 585
With water purify their hands, and take
The sacred off'ring of the salted cake;
While thus, with arms devoutly rais'd in air,
And solemn voice, the priest directs his pray'r:
    "God of the silver bow, thy ear incline,   590
Whose pow'r encircles Cilla the divine;
Whose sacred eye thy Tenedos surveys,
And gilds fair Chrysa with distinguish'd rays!
If, fir'd to vengeance at thy priest's request,
Thy direful darts inflict the raging pest;   595
Once more attend! avert the wasteful woe,
And smile propitious, and unbend thy bow."

So Chryses pray'd ; Apollo heard his pray'r :
And now the Greeks their hecatomb prepare ;
Between their horns the salted barley threw,   600
And with their heads to heav'n the victims slew :
The limbs they sever from th' inclosing hide ;
The thighs, selected to the gods, divide :
On these, in double cauls involv'd with art,
The choicest morsels lay from ev'ry part.   605
The priest himself before his altar stands,
And burns the off'ring with his holy hands,
Pours the black wine, and sees the flame aspire ;
The youths with instruments surround the fire :
The thighs thus sacrific'd, and entrails drest,   610
Th' assistants part, transfix, and roast the rest :
Then spread the tables, the repast prepare,
Each takes his seat, and each receives his share.
When now the rage of hunger was repress'd,
With pure libations they conclude the feast ;   615
The youths with wine the copious goblets crown'd,
And, pleas'd, dispense the flowing bowls around.
With hymns divine the joyous banquet ends,
The pæans lengthen'd till the sun descends :
The Greeks, restor'd, the grateful notes prolong :   620
Apollo listens, and approves the song.
  'T was night ; the chiefs beside their vessel lie,
Till rosy morn had purpled o'er the sky :
Then launch, and hoise the mast ; indulgent gales,
Supplied by Phœbus, fill the swelling sails ;   625
The milk-white canvas bellying as they blow,
The parted ocean foams and roars below :
Above the bounding billows swift they flew,
Till now the Grecian camp appear'd in view.
Far on the beach they haul their bark to land   630
(The crooked keel divides the yellow sand),

Then part, where stretch'd along the winding bay,
The ships and tents in mingled prospect lay.
   But, raging still, amidst his navy sate
The stern Achilles, steadfast in his hate; 635
Nor mix'd in combat nor in council join'd;
But wasting cares lay heavy on his mind:
In his black thoughts revenge and slaughter roll,
And scenes of blood rise dreadful in his soul.
   Twelve days were past, and now the dawning light 640
The gods had summon'd to th' Olympian height:
Jove, first ascending from the wat'ry bow'rs,
Leads the long order of æthereal pow'rs.
When, like the morning mist, in early day,
Rose from the flood the daughter of the sea; 645
And to the seats divine her flight address'd.
There, far apart, and high above the rest,
The Thund'rer sate ; where old Olympus shrouds
His hundred heads in heav'n, and props the clouds.
Suppliant the goddess stood: one hand she plac'd 650
Beneath his beard, and one his knees embrac'd.
" If e'er, O father of the gods ! " she said,
" My words could please thee, or my actions aid;
Some marks of honour on my son bestow,
And pay in glory what in life you owe. 655
Fame is at least by heav'nly promise due
To life so short, and now dishonour'd, too.
Avenge this wrong, O ever just and wise!
Let Greece be humbled, and the Trojans rise;
Till the proud king, and all th' Achaian race, 660
Shall heap with honours him they now disgrace."
   Thus Thetis spoke, but Jove in silence held
The sacred counsels of his breast conceal'd.
Not so repuls'd, the goddess closer press'd,
Still grasp'd his knees, and urg'd the dear request. 665

"O sire of gods and men! thy suppliant hear,
Refuse, or grant; for what has Jove to fear?
Or, oh! declare, of all the pow'rs above,
Is wretched Thetis least the care of Jove?"
   She said, and sighing thus the god replies,   670
Who rolls the thunder o'er the vaulted skies:
   "What hast thou ask'd? Ah! why should Jove engage
In foreign contests and domestic rage,
The gods' complaints, and Juno's fierce alarms,
While I, too partial, aid the Trojan arms?   675
Go, lest the haughty partner of my sway
With jealous eyes thy close access survey;
But part in peace, secure thy pray'r is sped:
Witness the sacred honours of our head,
The nod that ratifies the will divine,   680
The faithful, fix'd, irrevocable sign;
This seals thy suit, and this fulfils thy vows"—
He spoke, and awful bends his sable brows;
Shakes his ambrosial curls, and gives the nod,
The stamp of fate, and sanction of the god: 685
High heav'n with trembling the dread signal took,
And all Olympus to the centre shook.
   Swift to the seas profound the goddess flies,
Jove to his starry mansion in the skies.
The shining synod of th' immortals wait   690
The coming god, and from their thrones of state
Arising silent, rapt in holy fear,
Before the majesty of heav'n appear.
Trembling they stand, while Jove assumes the throne,
All but the god's imperious queen alone: 695
Late had she view'd the silver-footed dame,
And all her passions kindled into flame.
"Say, artful manager of heav'n," she cries,
"Who now partakes the secrets of the skies?

Thy Juno knows not the decrees of fate,   700
In vain the partner of imperial state.
What fav'rite goddess then those cares divides,
Which Jove in prudence from his consort hides?"
    To this the Thund'rer: " Seek not thou to find
The sacred counsels of almighty mind: 705
Involv'd in darkness lies the great decree,
Nor can the depths of fate be pierc'd by thee.
What fits thy knowledge, thou the first shalt know:
The first of gods above and men below:
But thou, nor they, shall search the thoughts that roll   710
Deep in the close recesses of my soul."
    Full on the sire, the goddess of the skies
Roll'd the large orbs of her majestic eyes,
And thus return'd: " Austere Saturnius, say,
From whence this wrath, or who controls thy sway?   715
Thy boundless will, for me, remains in force,
And all thy counsels take the destin'd course.
But 't is for Greece I fear: for late was seen
In close consult the silver-footed queen.
Jove to his Thetis nothing could deny,   720
Nor was the signal vain that shook the sky.
What fatal favour has the goddess won,
To grace her fierce inexorable son?
Perhaps in Grecian blood to drench the plain,
And glut his vengeance with my people slain."   725
    Then thus the god: " Oh restless fate of pride,
That strives to learn what heav'n resolves to hide;
Vain is the search, presumptuous and abhorr'd,
Anxious to thee, and odious to thy lord.
Let this suffice; th' immutable decree   730
No force can shake: what *is*, that *ought* to be.
Goddess, submit, nor dare our will withstand,
But dread the pow'r of this avenging hand;

Th' united strength of all the gods above
In vain resists th' omnipotence of Jove."   735
   The Thund'rer spoke, nor durst the queen reply;
A rev'rend horrour silenc'd all the sky.
The feast disturb'd, with sorrow Vulcan saw
His mother menac'd, and the gods in awe;
Peace at his heart, and pleasure his design,   740
Thus interpos'd the architect divine:
" The wretched quarrels of the mortal state
Are far unworthy, gods! of your debate:
Let men their days in senseless strife employ;
We, in eternal peace and constant joy.   745
Thou, goddess-mother, with our sire comply,
Nor break the sacred union of the sky:
Lest, rous'd to rage, he shake the blest abodes,
Launch the red lightning, and dethrone the gods.
If you submit, the Thund'rer stands appeas'd;   750
The gracious pow'r is willing to be pleas'd."
   Thus Vulcan spoke; and, rising with a bound,
The double bowl with sparkling nectar crown'd,
Which held to Juno in a cheerful way,
" Goddess," he cried, " be patient and obey.   755
Dear as you are, if Jove his arm extend,
I can but grieve, unable to defend.
What god so daring in your aid to move,
Or lift his hand against the force of Jove?
Once in your cause I felt his matchless might,   760
Hurl'd headlong downward from th' æthereal height;
Toss'd all the day in rapid circles round;
Nor, till the sun descended, touch'd the ground:
Breathless I fell, in giddy motion lost;
The Sinthians rais'd me on the Lemnian coast."   765
   He said, and to her hands the goblet heav'd,
Which, with a smile, the white-arm'd queen receiv'd.

Then to the rest he fill'd ; and, in his turn,
Each to his lips applied the nectar'd urn.
Vulcan with awkward grace his office plies,   770
And unextinguish'd laughter shakes the skies.
     Thus the blest gods the genial day prolong,
In feasts ambrosial and celestial song.
Apollo tun'd the lyre ; the muses round
With voice alternate aid the silver sound.   775
Meantime the radiant sun, to mortal sight
Descending swift, roll'd down the rapid light.
Then to their starry domes the gods depart,
The shining monuments of Vulcan's art :
Jove on his couch reclin'd his awful head,   780
And Juno slumber'd on the golden bed.

BOOK VI.

THE EPISODES OF GLAUCUS AND DIOMED, AND
OF HECTOR AND ANDROMACHE.

Now heav'n forsakes the fight; th' immortals yield
To human force and human skill the field:
Dark show'rs of jav'lins fly from foes to foes;
Now here, now there, the tide of combat flows;
While Troy's fam'd streams, that bound the deathful
    plain,   5
On either side run purple to the main.
  Great Ajax first to conquest led the way,
Broke the thick ranks, and turn'd the doubtful day.
The Thracian Acamas his falchion found,
And hew'd th' enormous giant to the ground;   10
His thund'ring arm a deadly stroke impress'd
Where the black horse-hair nodded o'er his crest:
Fix'd in his front the brazen weapon lies,
And seals in endless shades his swimming eyes.
  Next Teuthras' son distain'd the sands with blood,   15
Axylus, hospitable, rich, and good:
In fair Arisbe's walls (his native place)
He held his seat; a friend to human race.
Fast by the road, his ever-open door
Oblig'd the wealthy, and reliev'd the poor.   20
To stern Tydides now he falls a prey,
No friend to guard him in the dreadful day!
Breathless the good man fell, and by his side
His faithful servant, old Calesius, died.

By great Euryalus was Dresus slain,   25
And next he laid Opheltius on the plain.
Two twins were near, bold, beautiful, and young,
From a fair Naiad and Bucolion sprung
(Laomedon's white flocks Bucolion fed,
That monarch's first-born by a foreign bed;   30
In secret woods he won the Naiad's grace,
And two fair infants crown'd his strong embrace):
Here dead they lay in all their youthful charms;
The ruthless victor stripp'd their shining arms.
    Astyalus by Polypœtes fell;   35
Ulysses' spear Pidytes sent to hell;
By Teucer's shaft brave Aretaön bled,
And Nestor's son laid stern Ablerus dead;
Great Agamemnon, leader of the brave,
The mortal wound of rich Elatus gave,   40
Who held in Pedasus his proud abode,
And till'd the banks where silver Satnio flow'd.
Melanthius by Eurypylus was slain;
And Phylacus from Leitus flies in vain.
    Unbless'd Adrastus next at mercy lies   45
Beneath the Spartan spear, a living prize.
Scar'd with the din and tumult of the fight,
His headlong steeds, precipitate in flight,
Rush'd on a tamarisk's strong trunk, and broke
The shatter'd chariot from the crooked yoke: 50
Wide o'er the field, resistless as the wind,
For Troy they fly, and leave their lord behind.
Prone on his face he sinks beside the wheel:
Atrides o'er him shakes his vengeful steel;
The fallen chief in suppliant posture press'd   55
The victor's knees, and thus his prayer address'd:
    "Oh spare my youth, and for the life I owe
Large gifts of price my father shall bestow:

When fame shall tell that, not in battle slain,
Thy hollow ships his captive son detain,   60
Rich heaps of brass shall in thy tent be told,
And steel well-temper'd, and persuasive gold."
   He said : compassion touch'd the hero's heart ;
He stood suspended with the lifted dart :
As pity pleaded for his vanquish'd prize,   65
Stern Agamemnon swift to vengeance flies,
And furious thus: " O impotent of mind!
Shall these, shall these Atrides' mercy find?
Well hast thou known proud Troy's perfidious land,
And well her natives merit at thy hand!   70
Not one of all the race, nor sex, nor age,
Shall save a Trojan from our boundless rage :
Ilion shall perish whole, and bury all;
Her babes, her infants at the breast, shall fall,
A dreadful lesson of exampled fate,   75
To warn the nations, and to curb the great."
   The monarch spoke ; the words, with warmth address'd,
To rigid justice steel'd his brother's breast.
Fierce from his knees the hapless chief he thrust ;
The monarch's jav'lin stretch'd him in the dust.   80
Then, pressing with his foot his panting heart,
Forth from the slain he tugg'd the reeking dart.
Old Nestor saw, and rous'd the warriors' rage !
" Thus, heroes! thus the vig'rous combat wage!
No son of Mars descend, for servile gains,   85
To touch the booty, while a foe remains.
Behold yon glitt'ring host, your future spoil!
First gain the conquest, then reward the toil."
   And now had Greece eternal fame acquir'd,
And frighted Troy within her walls retir'd ;   90
Had not sage Helenus her state redress'd,
Taught by the gods that mov'd his sacred breast :

Where Hector stood, with great Æneas join'd,
The seer reveal'd the counsels of his mind:
  "Ye gen'rous chiefs! on whom th' immortals lay   95
The cares and glories of this doubtful day,
On whom your aids, your country's hopes depend,
Wise to consult, and active to defend!
Here, at our gates, your brave efforts unite,
Turn back the routed, and forbid the flight;   100
Ere yet their wives' soft arms the cowards gain,
The sport and insult of the hostile train.
When your commands have hearten'd every band,
Ourselves, here fix'd, will make the dang'rous stand;
Press'd as we are, and sore of former fight,   105
These straits demand our last remains of might.
Meanwhile, thou, Hector, to the town retire,
And teach our mother what the gods require:
Direct the queen to lead th' assembled train
Of Troy's chief matrons to Minerva's fane;   110
Unbar the sacred gates, and seek the pow'r
With offer'd vows, in Ilion's topmost tow'r.
The largest mantle her rich wardrobes hold,
Most priz'd for art, and labour'd o'er with gold,
Before the goddess' honour'd knees be spread;   115
And twelve young heifers to her altars led.
If so the pow'r, aton'd by fervent pray'r,
Our wives, our infants, and our city spare,
And far avert Tydides' wasteful ire,
That mows whole troops, and makes all Troy retire.   120
Not thus Achilles taught our hosts to dread,
Sprung tho' he was from more than mortal bed;
Not thus resistless rul'd the stream of fight,
In rage unbounded, and unmatch'd in might."
  Hector obedient heard; and, with a bound,   125
Leap'd from his trembling chariot to the ground;

Thro' all his host, inspiring force, he flies,
And bids the thunder of the battle rise.
With rage recruited the bold Trojans glow,
And turn the tide of conflict on the foe: 130
Fierce in the front he shakes two dazzling spears;
All Greece recedes, and midst her triumph fears:
Some god, they thought, who rul'd the fate of wars,
Shot down avenging, from the vault of stars.
    Then thus, aloud: " Ye dauntless Dardans, hear!   135
And you whom distant nations send to war;
Be mindful of the strength your fathers bore;
Be still yourselves, and Hector asks no more.
One hour demands me in the Trojan wall,
To bid our altars flame, and victims fall: 140
Nor shall, I trust, the matrons' holy train
And rev'rend elders seek the gods in vain."
    This said, with ample strides the hero pass'd;
The shield's large orb behind his shoulder cast,
His neck o'ershading, to his ancle hung;   145
And as he march'd the brazen buckler rung.
    Now paus'd the battle (godlike Hector gone),
When daring Glaucus and great Tydeus' son
Between both armies met; the chiefs from far
Observ'd each other, and had mark'd for war.   150
Near as they drew, Tydides thus began:
    "What art thou, boldest of the race of man?
Our eyes, till now, that aspect ne'er beheld,
Where fame is reap'd amid th' embattl'd field;
Yet far before the troops thou dar'st appear,   155
And meet a lance the fiercest heroes fear.
Unhappy they, and born of luckless sires,
Who tempt our fury when Minerva fires!
But if from heav'n, celestial thou descend,
Know, with immortals we no more contend.   160

Not long Lycurgus view'd the golden light,
That daring man who mix'd with gods in fight;
Bacchus, and Bacchus' votaries, he drove
With brandish'd steel from Nyssa's sacred grove;
Their consecrated spears lay scatter'd round,   165
With curling vines and twisted ivy bound;
While Bacchus headlong sought the briny flood,
And Thetis' arms receiv'd the trembling god.
Nor fail'd the crime th' immortals' wrath to move
(Th' immortals bless'd with endless ease above);   170
Depriv'd of sight, by their avenging doom,
Cheerless he breath'd, and wander'd in the gloom:
Then sunk unpitied to the dire abodes,
A wretch accurs'd, and hated by the gods!
I brave not heav'n; but if the fruits of earth   175
Sustain thy life, and human be thy birth,
Bold as thou art, too prodigal of breath,
Approach, and enter the dark gates of death."

  "What, or from whence I am, or who my sire,"
Replied the chief, "can Tydeus' son enquire?   180
Like leaves on trees the race of man is found,
Now green in youth, now with'ring on the ground:
Another race the following spring supplies,
They fall successive, and successive rise;
So generations in their course decay,   185
So flourish these, when those are pass'd away.
But if thou still persist to search my birth,
Then hear a tale that fills the spacious earth:
  "A city stands on Argos' utmost bound
(Argos the fair, for warlike steeds renown'd);   190
Æolian Sisyphus, with wisdom bless'd,
In ancient time the happy walls possess'd,
Then call'd Ephyre: Glaucus was his son;
Great Glaucus, father of Bellerophon,

Who o'er the sons of men in beauty shin'd,   195
Lov'd for that valor which preserves mankind.
Then mighty Prœtus Argos' sceptre sway'd,
Whose hard commands Bellerophon obey'd.
With direful jealousy the monarch rag'd,
And the brave prince in num'rous toils engag'd.   200
For him, Antea burn'd with lawless flame,
And strove to tempt him from the paths of fame :
In vain she tempted the relentless youth,
Endu'd with wisdom, sacred fear, and truth.
Fir'd at his scorn, the queen to Prœtus fled,   205
And begg'd revenge for her insulted bed :
Incens'd he heard, resolving on his fate ;
But hospitable laws restrain'd his hate :
To Lycia the devoted youth he sent,
With tablets seal'd, that told his dire intent.   210
Now, bless'd by ev'ry pow'r who guards the good,
The chief arriv'd at Xanthus' silver flood :
There Lycia's monarch paid him honours due ;
Nine days he feasted, and nine bulls he slew.
But when the tenth bright morning orient glow'd,   215
The faithful youth his monarch's mandate show'd :
The fatal tablets, till that instant seal'd,
The deathful secret to the king reveal'd.
First, dire Chimæra's conquest was enjoin'd ;
A mingled monster, of no mortal kind ;   220
Behind, a dragon's fiery tail was spread ;
A goat's rough body bore a lion's head ;
Her pitchy nostrils flaky flames expire ;
Her gaping throat emits infernal fire.
    " This pest he slaughter'd (for he read the skies,   225
And trusted heav'n's informing prodigies) ;
Then met in arms the Solymæan crew
(Fiercest of men), and those the warrior slew.

Next the bold Amazons' whole force defied ;
And conquer'd still, for heav'n was on his side.   230
    " Nor ended here his toils: his Lycian foes,
At his return, a treach'rous ambush rose,
With levell'd spears along the winding shore :
There fell they breathless, and return'd no more.
    " At length the monarch with repentant grief   235
Confess'd the gods, and god-descended chief :
His daughter gave, the stranger to detain,
With half the honours of his ample reign.
The Lycians grant a chosen space of ground,
With woods, with vineyards, and with harvests crown'd. 240
There long the chief his happy lot possess'd,
With two brave sons and one fair daughter bless'd
(Fair ev'n in heav'nly eyes : her fruitful love
Crown'd with Sarpedon's birth th' embrace of Jove).
But when at last, distracted in his mind,   245
Forsook by heav'n, forsaking human kind,
Wide o'er th' Aleian field he chose to stray,
A long, forlorn, uncomfortable way !
Woes heap'd on woes consum'd his wasted heart ;
His beauteous daughter fell by Phœbe's dart ;   250
His eldest-born by raging Mars was slain
In combat on the Solymæan plain.
Hippolochus surviv'd : from him I came,
The honour'd author of my birth and name ;
By his decree I sought the Trojan town,   255
By his instructions learn to win renown :
To stand the first in worth as in command,
To add new honours to my native land ;
Before my eyes my mighty sires to place,
And emulate the glories of our race."   260
    He spoke, and transport fill'd Tydides' heart ;
In earth the gen'rous warrior fix'd his dart,

Then friendly, thus, the Lycian prince address'd :
" Welcome, my brave hereditary guest !
Thus ever let us meet with kind embrace, 265
Nor stain the sacred friendship of our race.
Know, chief, our grandsires have been guests of old,
Œneus the strong, Bellerophon the bold ;
Our ancient seat his honour'd presence grac'd,
Where twenty days in genial rites he pass'd. 270
The parting heroes mutual presents left ;
A golden goblet was thy grandsire's gift :
Œneus a belt of matchless work bestow'd,
That rich with Tyrian dye refulgent glow'd
(This from his pledge I learn'd, which, safely stor'd 275
Among my treasures, still adorns my board :
For Tydeus left me young, when Thebe's wall
Beheld the sons of Greece untimely fall).
Mindful of this, in friendship let us join ;
If heav'n our steps to foreign lands incline, 280
My guest in Argos thou, and I in Lycia thine.
Enough of Trojans to this lance shall yield,
In the full harvest of yon ample field ;
Enough of Greeks shall dye thy spear with gore ;
But thou and Diomed be foes no more. 285
Now change we arms, and prove to either host
We guard the friendship of the line we boast.''
   Thus having said, the gallant chiefs alight,
Their hands they join, their mutual faith they plight ;
Brave Glaucus then each narrow thought resign'd 290
(Jove warm'd his bosom and enlarg'd his mind) ;
For Diomed's brass arms, of mean device,
For which nine oxen paid (a vulgar price),
He gave his own, of gold divinely wrought ;
A hundred beeves the shining purchase bought. 295
   Meantime the guardian of the Trojan state,

Great Hector, enter'd at the Scæan gate.
Beneath the beech-trees' consecrated shades,
The Trojan matrons and the Trojan maids
Around him flock'd, all press'd with pious care   300
For husbands, brothers, sons, engag'd in war.
He bids the train in long procession go,
And seek the gods, t' avert th' impending woe.
And now to Priam's stately courts he came,
Rais'd on arch'd columns of stupendous frame;   305
O'er these a range of marble structure runs;
The rich pavilions of his fifty sons,
In fifty chambers lodged : and rooms of state
Oppos'd to those, where Priam's daughters sate :
Twelve domes for them and their lov'd spouses shone,   310
Of equal beauty, and of polish'd stone.
Hither great Hector pass'd, nor pass'd unseen
Of royal Hecuba, his mother queen
(With her Laodice, whose beauteous face
Surpass'd the nymphs of Troy's illustrious race).   315
Long in a strict embrace she held her son,
And press'd his hand, and tender thus begun :
    "O Hector ! say, what great occasion calls
My son from fight, when Greece surrounds our walls?
Com'st thou to supplicate th' almighty pow'r,   320
With lifted hands from Ilion's lofty tow'r?
Stay, till I bring the cup with Bacchus crown'd,
In Jove's high name, to sprinkle on the ground,
And pay due vows to all the gods around.
Then with a plenteous draught refresh thy soul,   325
And draw new spirits from the gen'rous bowl;
Spent as thou art with long laborious fight,
The brave defender of thy country's right."
    " Far hence be Bacchus' gifts," the chief rejoin'd ;
" Inflaming wine, pernicious to mankind,   330

Unnerves the limbs, and dulls the noble mind.
Let chiefs abstain, and spare the sacred juice,
To sprinkle to the gods, its better use.
By me that holy office were profan'd ;
Ill fits it me, with human gore distain'd,   335
To the pure skies these horrid hands to raise,
Or offer heav'n's great sire polluted praise.
You, with your matrons, go, a spotless train !
And burn rich odours in Minerva's fane.
The largest mantle your full wardrobes hold,   340
Most priz'd for art, and labour'd o'er with gold,
Before the goddess' honour'd knees be spread,
And twelve young heifers to her altar led.
So may the pow'r, aton'd by fervent pray'r,
Our wives, our infants, and our city spare,   345
And far avert Tydides' wasteful ire,
Who mows whole troops, and makes all Troy retire.
Be this, O mother, your religious care ;
I go to rouse soft Paris to the war;
If yet, not lost to all the sense of shame,   350
The recreant warrior hear the voice of fame.
Oh would kind earth the hateful wretch embrace,
That pest of Troy, that ruin of our race !
Deep to the dark abyss might he descend,
Troy yet should flourish, and my sorrows end."   355
     This heard, she gave command ; and summon'd came
Each noble matron and illustrious dame.
The Phrygian queen to her rich wardrobe went,
Where treasur'd odours breath'd a costly scent.
There lay the vestures of no vulgar art,   360
Sidonian maids embroider'd ev'ry part,
Whom from soft Sidon youthful Paris bore,
With Helen touching on the Tyrian shore.
Here as the queen revolv'd with careful eyes

The various textures and the various dyes,   365
She chose a veil that shone superior far,
And glow'd refulgent as the morning star.
Herself with this the long procession leads;
The train majestically slow proceeds.
Soon as to Ilion's topmost tow'r they come,   370
And awful reach the high Palladian dome,
Antenor's consort, fair Theano, waits
As Pallas' priestess, and unbars the gates.
With hands uplifted, and imploring eyes,
They fill the dome with supplicating cries.   375
The priestess then the shining veil displays,
Plac'd on Minerva's knees, and thus she prays:
    " O awful goddess! ever-dreadful maid,
Troy's strong defence, unconquer'd Pallas, aid!
Break thou Tydides' spear, and let him fall   380
Prone on the dust before the Trojan wall.
So twelve young heifers, guiltless of the yoke,
Shall fill thy temple with a grateful smoke.
But thou, aton'd by penitence and pray'r,
Ourselves, our infants, and our city spare!"   385
So pray'd the priestess in her holy fane;
So vow'd the matrons, but they vow'd in vain.
    While these appear before the pow'r with pray'rs,
Hector to Paris' lofty dome repairs.
Himself the mansion rais'd, from ev'ry part   390
Assembling architects of matchless art.
Near Priam's court and Hector's palace stands
The pompous structure, and the town commands.
A spear the hero bore of wond'rous strength,
Of full ten cubits was the lance's length;   395
The steely point with golden ringlets join'd,
Before him brandish'd, at each motion shin'd.
Thus ent'ring, in the glitt'ring rooms he found

His brother-chief, whose useless arms lay round,
His eyes delighting with their splendid show,   400
Bright'ning the shield, and polishing the bow.
Beside him Helen with her virgins stands,
Guides their rich labours, and instructs their hands.
   Him thus unactive, with an ardent look
The prince beheld, and high-resenting spoke :   405
" Thy hate to Troy is this the time to show
(O wretch ill-fated, and thy country's foe) ?
Paris and Greece against us both conspire,
Thy close resentment, and their vengeful ire ;
For thee great Ilion's guardian heroes fall,   410
Till heaps of dead alone defend her wall ;
For thee the soldier bleeds, the matron mourns,
And wasteful war in all its fury burns.
Ungrateful man ! deserves not this thy care,
Our troops to hearten, and our toils to share ?   415
Rise, or behold the conqu'ring flames ascend,
And all the Phrygian glories at an end."
   " Brother, 't is just," replied the beauteous youth,
"Thy free remonstrance proves thy worth and truth :
Yet charge my absence less, O gen'rous chief !   420
On hate to Troy, than conscious shame and grief.
Here, hid from human eyes, thy brother sate,
And mourn'd in secret his and Ilion's fate.
'T is now enough : now glory spreads her charms,
And beauteous Helen calls her chief to arms.   425
Conquest to-day my happier sword may bless,
'T is man's to fight, but heav'n's to give success.
But while I arm, contain thy ardent mind ;
Or go, and Paris shall not lag behind."
   He said, nor answer'd Priam's warlike son ;   430
When Helen thus with lowly grace begun :
" O gen'rous brother ! if the guilty dame

That caus'd these woes deserve a sister's name !
Would heav'n, ere all these dreadful deeds were done,
The day that show'd me to the golden sun   435
Had seen my death! Why did not whirlwinds bear
The fatal infant to the fowls of air?
Why sunk I not beneath the whelming tide,
And midst the roarings of the waters died?
Heav'n fill'd up all my ills, and I accurs'd   440
Bore all, and Paris of those ills the worst.
Helen at least a braver spouse might claim,
Warm'd with some virtue, some regard of fame !
Now, tir'd with toils, thy fainting limbs recline,
With toils sustain'd for Paris' sake and mine :   445
The gods have link'd our miserable doom,
Our present woe and infamy to come :
Wide shall it spread, and last thro' ages long,
Example sad ! and theme of future song."
   The chief replied: "This time forbids to rest :   450
The Trojan bands, by hostile fury press'd,
Demand their Hector, and his arm require ;
The combat urges, and my soul's on fire.
Urge thou thy knight to march where glory calls,
And timely join me, ere I leave the walls.   455
Ere yet I mingle in the direful fray,
My wife, my infant, claim a moment's stay :
This day (perhaps the last that sees me here)
Demands a parting word, a tender tear :
This day some god, who hates our Trojan land,   460
May vanquish Hector by a Grecian hand."
   He said, and pass'd with sad presaging heart,
To seek his spouse, his soul's far dearer part ;
At home he sought her, but he sought in vain :
She, with one maid of all her menial train,   465
Had thence retir'd ; and, with her second joy,

The young Astyanax, the hope of Troy,
Pensive she stood on Ilion's tow'ry height,
Beheld the war, and sicken'd at the sight;
There her sad eyes in vain her lord explore, 470
Or weep the wounds her bleeding country bore.
But he who found not whom his soul desir'd,
Whose virtue charm'd him as her beauty fir'd,
Stood in the gates, and ask'd what way she bent
Her parting step; if to the fane she went, 475
Where late the mourning matrons made resort;
Or sought her sisters in the Trojan court.
" Not to the court," replied th' attendant train,
" Nor, mix'd with matrons, to Minerva's fane:
To Ilion's steepy tow'r she bent her way, 480
To mark the fortunes of the doubtful day.
Troy fled, she heard, before the Grecian sword:
She heard, and trembled for her distant lord;
Distracted with surprise, she seem'd to fly,
Fear on her cheek, and sorrow in her eye. 485
The nurse attended with her infant boy,
The young Astyanax, the hope of Troy."
Hector, this heard, return'd without delay;
Swift thro' the town he trod his former way,
Thro' streets of palaces and walks of state; 490
And met the mourner at the Scæan gate.
With haste to meet him sprung the joyful fair,
His blameless wife, Eëtion's wealthy heir
(Cilician Thebe great Eëtion sway'd,
And Hippoplacus' wide-extended shade): 495
The nurse stood near, in whose embraces press'd,
His only hope hung smiling at her breast,
Whom each soft charm and early grace adorn,
Fair as the new-born star that gilds the morn.
To this lov'd infant Hector gave the name 500

Scamandrius, from Scamander's honour'd stream:
Astyanax the Trojans call'd the boy,
From his great father, the defence of Troy.
Silent the warrior smil'd, and, pleas'd, resign'd
To tender passions all his mighty mind: 505
His beauteous princess cast a mournful look,
Hung on his hand, and then dejected spoke;
Her bosom labour'd with a boding sigh,
And the big tear stood trembling in her eye.
  "Too daring prince! ah whither dost thou run?   510
Ah too forgetful of thy wife and son!
And think'st thou not how wretched we shall be,
A widow I, a helpless orphan he!
For sure such courage length of life denies,
And thou must fall, thy virtue's sacrifice.   515
Greece in her single heroes strove in vain;
Now hosts oppose thee, and thou must be slain!
Oh grant me, gods! ere Hector meets his doom,
All I can ask of heav'n, an early tomb!
So shall my days in one sad tenour run,   520
And end with sorrows as they first begun.
No parent now remains, my griefs to share,
No father's aid, no mother's tender care.
The fierce Achilles wrapt our walls in fire,
Laid Thebe waste, and slew my warlike sire!   525
His fate compassion in the victor bred;
Stern as he was, he yet rever'd the dead,
His radiant arms preserv'd from hostile spoil,
And laid him decent on the fun'ral pile;
Then rais'd a mountain where his bones were burn'd; 530
The mountain nymphs the rural tomb adorn'd;
Jove's sylvan daughters bade their elms bestow
A barren shade, and in his honour grow.
  "By the same arm my sev'n brave brothers fell;

In one sad day beheld the gates of hell ; 535
While the fat herds and snowy flocks they fed,
Amid their fields the hapless heroes bled!
My mother liv'd to bear the victor's bands,
The queen of Hippoplacia's sylvan lands :
Redeem'd too late, she scarce beheld again 540
Her pleasing empire and her native plain,
When, ah! oppress'd by life-consuming woe,
She fell a victim to Diana's bow.
  " Yet while my Hector still survives, I see
My father, mother, brethren, all, in thee. 545
Alas! my parents, brothers, kindred, all,
Once more will perish if my Hector fall.
Thy wife, thy infant, in thy danger share ;
Oh prove a husband's and a father's care !
That quarter most the skilful Greeks annoy, 550
Where yon wild fig-trees join the wall of Troy :
Thou, from this tow'r defend th' important post ;
There Agamemnon points his dreadful host,
That pass Tydides, Ajax, strive to gain,
And there the vengeful Spartan fires his train. 555
Thrice our bold foes the fierce attack have giv'n,
Or led by hopes, or dictated from heav'n.
Let others in the field their arms employ,
But stay my Hector here, and guard his Troy."
  The chief replied: " That post shall be my care, 560
Nor that alone, but all the works of war.
How would the sons of Troy, in arms renown'd,
And Troy's proud dames, whose garments sweep the
      ground,
Attaint the lustre of my former name,
Should Hector basely quit the field of fame? 565
My early youth was bred to martial pains,
My soul impels me to th' embattl'd plains :

Let me be foremost to defend the throne,
And guard my father's glories, and my own.
Yet come it will, the day decreed by fates   570
(How my heart trembles while my tongue relates!);
The day when thou, imperial Troy! must bend,
And see thy warriors fall, thy glories end.
And yet no dire presage so wounds my mind,
My mother's death, the ruin of my kind,   575
Not Priam's hoary hairs defil'd with gore,
Not all my brothers gasping on the shore;
As thine, Andromache! thy griefs I dread;
I see thee trembling, weeping, captive led!
In Argive looms our battles to design,   580
And woes of which so large a part was thine!
To bear the victor's hard commands, or bring
The weight of waters from Hyperia's spring.
There, while you groan beneath the load of life,
They cry, 'Behold the mighty Hector's wife!'   585
Some haughty Greek, who lives thy tears to see,
Embitters all thy woes by naming me.
The thoughts of glory past, and present shame,
A thousand griefs, shall waken at the name!
May I lie cold before that dreadful day,   590
Press'd with a load of monumental clay!
Thy Hector, wrapp'd in everlasting sleep,
Shall neither hear thee sigh, nor see thee weep."
    Thus having spoke, th' illustrious chief of Troy
Stretch'd his fond arms to clasp the lovely boy.   595
The babe clung crying to his nurse's breast,
Scar'd at the dazzling helm, and nodding crest.
With secret pleasure each fond parent smil'd,
And Hector hasted to relieve his child;
The glitt'ring terrors from his brows unbound,   600
And placed the beaming helmet on the ground.

Then kiss'd the child. and, lifting high in air,
Thus to the gods preferr'd a father's pray'r:
　"O thou whose glory fills th' æthereal throne,
And all ye deathless powers! protect my son!　605
Grant him, like me, to purchase just renown,
To guard the Trojans, to defend the crown,
Against his country's foes the war to wage,
And rise the Hector of the future age!
So when, triumphant from successful toils,　610
Of heroes slain he bears the reeking spoils,
Whole hosts may hail him with deserv'd acclaim,
And say, 'This chief transcends his father's fame':
While pleas'd, amidst the gen'ral shouts of Troy,
His mother's conscious heart o'erflows with joy."　615
　He spoke, and fondly gazing on her charms,
Restor'd the pleasing burthen to her arms;
Soft on her fragrant breast the babe she laid,
Hush'd to repose, and with a smile survey'd.
The troubled pleasure soon chastis'd by fear,　620
She mingled with the smile a tender tear.
The soften'd chief with kind compassion view'd,
And dried the falling drops, and thus pursu'd:
　"Andromache! my soul's far better part,
Why with untimely sorrows heaves thy heart?　625
No hostile hand can antedate my doom,
Till fate condemns me to the silent tomb.
Fix'd is the term to all the race of earth,
And such the hard condition of our birth.
No force can then resist, no flight can save;　630
All sink alike, the fearful and the brave.
No more — but hasten to thy tasks at home,
There guide the spindle, and direct the loom:
Me glory summons to the martial scene;
The field of combat is the sphere for men.　635

Where heroes war, the foremost place I claim,
The first in danger as the first in fame."
   Thus having said, the glorious chief resumes
His tow'ry helmet, black with shading plumes.
His princess parts with a prophetic sigh,   640
Unwilling parts, and oft reverts her eye,
That stream'd at ev'ry look: then, moving slow,
Sought her own palace, and indulg'd her woe.
There, while her tears deplor'd the godlike man,
Thro' all her train the soft infection ran;   645
The pious maids their mingled sorrows shed,
And mourn the living Hector as the dead.
   But now, no longer deaf to honour's call,
Forth issues Paris from the palace wall.
In brazen arms that cast a gleamy ray,   650
Swift thro' the town the warrior bends his way.
The wanton courser thus, with reins unbound,
Breaks from his stall, and beats the trembling ground;
Pamper'd and proud he seeks the wonted tides,
And laves, in height of blood, his shining sides: 655
His head now freed he tosses to the skies;
His mane dishevell'd o'er his shoulders flies;
He snuffs the females in the distant plain,
And springs, exulting, to his fields again.
With equal triumph, sprightly, bold, and gay, 660
In arms refulgent as the god of day,
The son of Priam, glorying in his might,
Rush'd forth with Hector to the fields of fight.
And now the warriors passing on the way,
The graceful Paris first excus'd his stay.   665
To whom the noble Hector thus replied:
"O chief! in blood, and now in arms, allied!
Thy pow'r in war with justice none contest;
Known is thy courage, and thy strength confess'd.

What pity, sloth should seize a soul so brave,   670
Or godlike Paris live a woman's slave !
My heart weeps blood at what the Trojans say,
And hopes thy deeds shall wipe the stain away.
Haste then, in all their glorious labours share ;
For much they suffer, for thy sake, in war.   675
These ills shall cease, whene'er by Jove's decree
We crown the bowl to Heav'n and Liberty :
While the proud foe his frustrate triumphs mourns,
And Greece indignant thro' her seas returns."

BOOK XXII.

THE DEATH OF HECTOR.

Thus to their bulwarks, smit with panic fear,
The herded Ilians rush like driven deer;
There safe, they wipe the briny drops away,
And drown in bowls the labours of the day.
Close to the walls, advancing o'er the fields,   5
Beneath one roof of well-compacted shields,
March, bending on, the Greeks' embodied pow'rs,
Far-stretching in the shade of Trojan tow'rs.
Great Hector singly stay'd; chain'd down by fate,
There fix'd he stood before the Scæan gate;   10
Still his bold arms determin'd to employ,
The guardian still of long-defended Troy.
   Apollo now to tir'd Achilles turns
(The pow'r confess'd in all his glory burns),
"And what," he cries, "has Peleus' son in view,   15
With mortal speed a godhead to pursue?
For not to thee to know the gods is giv'n,
Unskill'd to trace the latent marks of heav'n.
What boots thee now that Troy forsook the plain?
Vain thy past labour, and thy present vain: 20
Safe in their walls are now her troops bestow'd,
While here thy frantic rage attacks a god."
   The chief incens'd: "Too partial god of day!
To check my conquests in the middle way:
How few in Ilion else had refuge found!   25
What gasping numbers now had bit the ground!
46

Thou robb'st me of a glory justly mine,
Pow'rful of godhead, and of fraud divine :
Mean fame, alas ! for one of heav'nly strain,
To cheat a mortal who repines in vain." 30
   Then to the city, terrible and strong,
With high and haughty steps he tower'd along :
So the proud courser, victor of the prize,
To the near goal with double ardour flies.
Him, as he blazing shot across the field, 35
The careful eyes of Priam first beheld.
Not half so dreadful rises to the sight,
Thro' the thick gloom of some tempestuous night,
Orion's dog (the year when autumn weighs),
And o'er the feebler stars exerts his rays ; 40
Terrific glory ! for his burning breath
Taints the red air with fevers, plagues, and death.
So flam'd his fiery mail.   Then wept the sage :
He strikes his rev'rend head, now white with age ;
He lifts his wither'd arms ; obtests the skies ; 45
He calls his much-lov'd son with feeble cries :
The son, resolv'd Achilles' force to dare,
Full at the Scæan gate expects the war :
While the sad father on the rampart stands,
And thus adjures him with extended hands : 50
   "Ah stay not, stay not ! guardless and alone ;
Hector, my lov'd, my dearest, bravest son !
Methinks already I behold thee slain,
And stretch'd beneath that fury of the plain.
Implacable Achilles ! might'st thou be 55
To all the gods no dearer than to me !
Thee vultures wild should scatter round the shore,
And bloody dogs grow fiercer from thy gore !
How many valiant sons I late enjoy'd,
Valiant in vain ! by thy curs'd arm destroy'd : 60

Or, worse than slaughter'd, sold in distant isles
To shameful bondage and unworthy toils.
Two, while I speak, my eyes in vain explore,
Two from one mother sprung, my Polydore
And lov'd Lycaon; now perhaps no more!　　　　　65
Oh! if in yonder hostile camp they live,
What heaps of gold, what treasures would I give
(Their grandsire's wealth, by right of birth their own,
Consign'd his daughter with Lelegia's throne):
But if (which heav'n forbid) already lost,　　　　　70
All pale they wander on the Stygian coast,
What sorrows then must their sad mother know,
What anguish I! unutterable woe!
Yet less that anguish, less to her, to me,
Less to all Troy, if not depriv'd of thee.　　　　　75
Yet shun Achilles! enter yet the wall;
And spare thyself, thy father, spare us all!
Save thy dear life: or if a soul so brave
Neglect that thought, thy dearer glory save.
Pity, while yet I live, these silver hairs;　　　　　80
While yet thy father feels the woes he bears,
Yet curs'd with sense! a wretch, whom in his rage
(All trembling on the verge of helpless age)
Great Jove has plac'd, sad spectacle of pain!
The bitter dregs of fortune's cup to drain:　　　　　85
To fill with scenes of death his closing eyes,
And number all his days by miseries!
My heroes slain, my bridal bed o'erturn'd,
My daughters ravish'd, and my city burn'd,
My bleeding infants dash'd against the floor;　　　　　90
These I have yet to see, perhaps yet more!
Perhaps ev'n I, reserv'd by angry fate
The last sad relic of my ruin'd state
(Dire pomp of sov'reign wretchedness!), must fall

And stain the pavement of my regal hall; 95
Where famish'd dogs, late guardians of my door,
Shall lick their mangled master's spatter'd gore.
Yet for my sons I thank ye, gods! 't was well:
Well have they perish'd, for in fight they fell.
Who dies in youth and vigour, dies the best, 100
Struck thro' with wounds, all honest on the breast.
But when the fates, in fulness of their rage,
Spurn the hoar head of unresisting age,
In dust the rev'rend lineaments deform,
And pour to dogs the life-blood scarcely warm; 105
This, this is misery! the last, the worst,
That man can feel: man, fated to be curs'd!"
   He said, and acting what no words could say,
Rent from his head the silver locks away.
With him the mournful mother bears a part: 110
Yet all their sorrows turn not Hector's heart:
The zone unbrac'd, her bosom she display'd;
And thus, fast-falling the salt tears, she said:
   "Have mercy on me, O my son! revere
The words of age; attend a parent's pray'r! 115
If ever thee in these fond arms I press'd,
Or still'd thy infant clamours at this breast;
Ah! do not thus our helpless years forego,
But, by our walls secur'd, repel the foe.
Against his rage if singly thou proceed, 120
Should'st thou (but heav'n avert it!), should'st thou
    bleed,
Nor must thy corse lie honour'd on the bier,
Nor spouse, nor mother, grace thee with a tear;
Far from our pious rites, those dear remains
Must feast the vultures on the naked plains." 125
   So they, while down their cheeks the torrents roll:
But fix'd remains the purpose of his soul;

Resolv'd he stands, and with a fiery glance
Expects the hero's terrible advance.
So, roll'd up in his den, the swelling snake   130
Beholds the traveller approach the brake;
When, fed with noxious herbs, his turgid veins
Have gather'd half the poisons of the plains;
He burns, he stiffens with collected ire,
And his red eyeballs glare with living fire.   135
Beneath a turret, on his shield reclin'd,
He stood, and question'd thus his mighty mind:
    "Where lies my way?   To enter in the wall?
Honour and shame th' ungen'rous thought recall:
Shall proud Polydamas before the gate   140
Proclaim his counsels are obey'd too late,
Which timely follow'd but the former night,
What numbers had been sav'd by Hector's flight?
That wise advice rejected with disdain,
I feel my folly in my people slain.   145
Methinks my suff'ring country's voice I hear,
But most, her worthless sons insult my ear,
On my rash courage charge the chance of war,
And blame those virtues which they cannot share.
No — if I e'er return, return I must   150
Glorious, my country's terror laid in dust:
Or if I perish, let her see me fall
In field at least, and fighting for her wall.
And yet suppose these measures I forego,
Approach unarm'd, and parley with the foe,   155
The warrior-shield, the helm, and lance lay down,
And treat on terms of peace to save the town:
The wife withheld, the treasure ill-detain'd
(Cause of the war, and grievance of the land),
With honourable justice to restore;   160
And add half Ilion's yet remaining store,

Which Troy shall, sworn, produce ; that injur'd Greece
May share our wealth, and leave our walls in peace.
But why this thought ? Unarm'd if I should go,
What hope of mercy from this vengeful foe,   165
But woman-like to fall, and fall without a blow ?
We greet not here as man conversing man,
Met at an oak or journeying o'er a plain ;
No season now for calm, familiar talk,
Like youths and maidens in an ev'ning walk :   170
War is our business, but to whom is giv'n
To die or triumph, that determine heav'n ! "
   Thus pond'ring, like a god the Greek drew nigh :
His dreadful plumage nodded from on high ;
The Pelian jav'lin, in his better hand,   175
Shot trembling rays that glitter'd o'er the land ;
And on his breast the beamy splendours shone
Like Jove's own light'ning, or the rising sun.
As Hector sees, unusual terrors rise,
Struck by some god, he fears, recedes, and flies :   180
He leaves the gates, he leaves the walls behind ;
Achilles follows like the winged wind.
Thus at the panting dove the falcon flies
(The swiftest racer of the liquid skies) ;
Just when he holds, or thinks he holds, his prey,   185
Obliquely wheeling thro' th' aërial way,
With open beak and shrilling cries he springs,
And aims his claws, and shoots upon his wings :
No less fore-right the rapid chase they held,
One urg'd by fury, one by fear impell'd ;   190
Now circling round the walls their course maintain,
Where the high watch-tow'r overlooks the plain ;
Now where the fig-trees spread their umbrage broad
(A wider compass), smoke along the road.
Next by Scamander's double source they bound,   195

Where two fam'd fountains burst the parted ground :
This hot thro' scorching clefts is seen to rise,
With exhalations steaming to the skies ;
That the green banks in summer's heat o'erflows,
Like crystal clear, and cold as winter snows.   200
Each gushing fount a marble cistern fills,
Whose polish'd bed receives the falling rills ;
Where Trojan dames (ere yet alarm'd by Greece)
Wash'd their fair garments in the days of peace.
By these they pass'd, one chasing, one in flight   205
(The mighty fled, pursu'd by stronger might) ;
Swift was the course ; no vulgar prize they play,
No vulgar victim must reward the day
(Such as in races crown the speedy strife) :
The prize contended was great Hector's life.   210
    As when some hero's fun'rals are decreed,
In grateful honour of the mighty dead ;
Where high rewards the vig'rous youth inflame
(Some golden tripod, or some lovely dame),
The panting coursers swiftly turn the goal,   215
And with them turns the rais'd spectator's soul :
Thus three times round the Trojan wall they fly ;
The gazing gods lean forward from the sky :
To whom, while eager on the chase they look,
The sire of mortals and immortals spoke :   220
    " Unworthy sight ! the man belov'd of heav'n,
Behold, inglorious round yon city driv'n !
My heart partakes the gen'rous Hector's pain ;
Hector, whose zeal whole hecatombs has slain,
Whose grateful fumes the gods receiv'd with joy,   225
From Ida's summits and the tow'rs of Troy :
Now see him flying ! to his fears resign'd,
And Fate and fierce Achilles close behind.
Consult, ye pow'rs ('t is worthy your debate),

Whether to snatch him from impending fate, 230
Or let him bear, by stern Pelides slain
(Good as he is), the lot impos'd on man?"
   Then Pallas thus: "Shall he whose vengeance forms
      forms
The forky bolt, and blackens heav'n with storms,
Shall he prolong one Trojan's forfeit breath, 235
A man, a mortal, pre-ordain'd to death?
And will no murmurs fill the courts above?
No gods indignant blame their partial Jove?"
   "Go then," return'd the sire, "without delay;
Exert thy will : I give the fates their way." 240
Swift at the mandate pleas'd Tritonia flies,
And stoops impetuous from the cleaving skies.
   As thro' the forest, o'er the vale and lawn,
The well-breath'd beagle drives the flying fawn;
In vain he tries the covert of the brakes, 245
Or deep beneath the trembling thicket shakes:
Sure of the vapour in the tainted dews,
The certain hound his various maze pursues :
Thus step by step, where'er the Trojan wheel'd,
There swift Achilles compass'd round the field. 250
Oft as to reach the Dardan gates he bends,
And hopes th' assistance of his pitying friends
(Whose show'ring arrows, as he cours'd below,
From the high turrets might oppress the foe),
So oft Achilles turns him to the plain: 255
He eyes the city, but he eyes in vain.
As men in slumbers seem with speedy pace
One to pursue, and one to lead the chase,
Their sinking limbs the fancied course forsake,
Nor this can fly, nor that can overtake : 260
No less the lab'ring heroes pant and strain;
While that but flies, and this pursues, in vain.

What god, O Muse ! assisted Hector's force,
With fate itself so long to hold the course !
Phœbus it was: who, in his latest hour,   265
Endu'd his knees with strength, his nerves with pow'r.
And great Achilles, lest some Greek's advance
Should snatch the glory from his lifted lance,
Sign'd to the troops, to yield his foe the way,
And leave untouch'd the honours of the day.   270
    Jove lifts the golden balances, that show
The fates of mortal men and things below:
Here each contending hero's lot he tries,
And weighs, with equal hand, their destinies.
Low sinks the scale surcharg'd with Hector's fate;   275
Heavy with death it sinks, and hell receives the weight.
    Then Phœbus left him.   Fierce Minerva flies
To stern Pelides, and, triumphing, cries :
" O lov'd of Jove ! this day our labours cease,
And conquest blazes with full beams on Greece.   280
Great Hector falls; that Hector fam'd so far,
Drunk with renown, insatiable of war,
Falls by thy hand and mine ! nor force nor flight
Shall more avail him, nor his god of light.
See, where in vain he supplicates above,   285
Roll'd at the feet of unrelenting Jove !
Rest here : myself will lead the Trojan on,
And urge to meet the fate he cannot shun."
    Her voice divine the chief with joyful mind
Obey'd ; and rested, on his lance reclin'd ;   290
While like Deïphobus the martial dame
(Her face, her gesture, and her arms, the same),
In show an aid, by hapless Hector's side
Approach'd, and greets him thus with voice belied :
    " Too long, O Hector ! have I borne the sight   295
Of this distress, and sorrow'd in thy flight :

It fits us now a noble stand to make,
And here, as brothers, equal fates partake."
    Then he: "O prince! allied in blood and fame,
Dearer than all that own a brother's name;   300
Of all that Hecuba to Priam bore,
Long tried, long lov'd; much lov'd, but honour'd more!
Since you of all our num'rous race alone
Defend my life, regardless of your own."
    Again the goddess: "Much my father's pray'r,   305
And much my mother's, press'd me to forbear:
My friends embrac'd my knees, adjur'd my stay,
But stronger love impell'd, and I obey.
Come then, the glorious conflict let us try,
Let the steel sparkle and the jav'lin fly;   310
Or let us stretch Achilles on the field,
Or to his arm our bloody trophies yield."
    Fraudful she said; then swiftly march'd before;
The Dardan hero shuns his foe no more.
Sternly they met.   The silence Hector broke;   315
His dreadful plumage nodded as he spoke:
    "Enough, O son of Peleus! Troy has view'd
Her walls thrice circled, and her chief pursu'd.
But now some god within me bids me try
Thine or my fate: I kill thee or I die.   320
Yet on the verge of battle let us stay,
And for a moment's space suspend the day:
Let heav'n's high pow'rs be call'd to arbitrate
The just conditions of this stern debate
(Eternal witnesses of all below,   325
And faithful guardians of the treasur'd vow!):
To them I swear: if, victor in the strife,
Jove by these hands shall shed thy noble life,
No vile dishonour shall thy corse pursue;
Stripp'd of its arms alone (the conqu'ror's due),   330

The rest to Greece uninjur'd I 'll restore :
Now plight thy mutual oath, I ask no more."
    " Talk not of oaths," the dreadful chief replies,
While anger flash'd from his disdainful eyes,
" Detested as thou art, and ought to be,   335
Nor oath nor pact Achilles plights with thee ;
Such pacts as lambs and rabid wolves combine,
Such leagues as men and furious lions join,
To such I call the gods ! one constant state
Of lasting rancour and eternal hate :   340
No thought but rage, and never-ceasing strife,
Till death extinguish rage, and thought, and life.
Rouse then thy forces this important hour,
Collect thy soul, and call forth all thy pow'r.
No farther subterfuge, no farther chance ;   345
'T is Pallas, Pallas gives thee to my lance.
Each Grecian ghost by thee depriv'd of breath,
Now hovers round, and calls thee to thy death."
    He spoke, and launch'd his jav'lin at the foe ;
But Hector shunn'd the meditated blow :   350
He stoop'd, while o'er his head the flying spear
Sung innocent, and spent its force in air.
Minerva watch'd it falling on the land,
Then drew, and gave to great Achilles' hand,
Unseen of Hector, who, elate with joy,   355
Now shakes his lance, and braves the dread of Troy :
    " The life you boasted to that jav'lin giv'n,
Prince ! you have miss'd.   My fate depends on heav'n.
To thee (presumptuous as thou art) unknown
Or what must prove my fortune or thy own.   360
Boasting is but an art, our fears to blind,
And with false terrors sink another's mind.
But know, whatever fate I am to try,
By no dishonest wound shall Hector die ;

I shall not fall a fugitive at least,   365
My soul shall bravely issue from my breast.
But first, try thou my arm ; and may this dart
End all my country's woes, deep buried in thy heart !"
 The weapon flew, its course unerring held ;
Unerring, but the heav'nly shield repell'd   370
The mortal dart; resulting with a bound
From off the ringing orb, it struck the ground.
Hector beheld his jav'lin fall in vain,
Nor other lance nor other hope remain;
He calls Deïphobus, demands a spear,   375
In vain, for no Deïphobus was there.
All comfortless he stands ; then, with a sigh :
"'T is so — heav'n wills it, and my hour is nigh !
I deem'd Deïphobus had heard my call,
But he secure lies guarded in the wall.   380
A god deceiv'd me ; Pallas, 't was thy deed :
Death and black fate approach ! 'T is I must bleed.
No refuge now, no succour from above,
Great Jove deserts me, and the son of Jove,
Propitious once and kind ! Then welcome fate !   385
'T is true I perish, yet I perish great :
Yet in a mighty deed I shall expire,
Let future ages hear it, and admire !"
 Fierce, at the word, his weighty sword he drew,
And, all collected, on Achilles flew.   390
So Jove's bold bird, high balanc'd in the air,
Stoops from the clouds to truss the quiv'ring hare.
Nor less Achilles his fierce soul prepares ;
Before his breast the flaming shield he bears,
Refulgent orb ! above his fourfold cone   395
The gilded horse-hair sparkled in the sun,
Nodding at ev'ry step (Vulcanian frame !),
And as he mov'd, his figure seem'd on flame.

As radiant Hesper shines with keener light,
Far-beaming o'er the silver host of night,   400
When all the starry train emblaze the sphere:
So shone the point of great Achilles' spear.
In his right hand he waves the weapon round,
Eyes the whole man, and meditates the wound:
But the rich mail Patroclus lately wore,   405
Securely cas'd the warrior's body o'er.
One place at length he spies, to let in fate,
Where 'twixt the neck and throat the jointed plate
Gave entrance: thro' that penetrable part
Furious he drove the well-directed dart: 410
Nor pierc'd the windpipe yet, nor took the pow'r
Of speech, unhappy! from thy dying hour.
Prone on the field the bleeding warrior lies,
While thus, triumphing, stern Achilles cries:

    "At last is Hector stretch'd upon the plain,   415
Who fear'd no vengeance for Patroclus slain:
Then, prince! you should have fear'd what now you feel;
Achilles absent was Achilles still.
Yet a short space the great avenger stay'd,
Then low in dust thy strength and glory laid.   420
Peaceful he sleeps, with all our rites adorn'd,
For ever honour'd, and for ever mourn'd:
While, cast to all the rage of hostile pow'r,
Thee birds shall mangle, and the dogs devour."

    Then Hector, fainting at th' approach of death: 425
"By thy own soul! by those who gave thee breath!
By all the sacred prevalence of pray'r;
Ah, leave me not for Grecian dogs to tear!
The common rites of sepulture bestow,
To soothe a father's and a mother's woe;   430
Let their large gifts procure an urn at least,
And Hector's ashes in his country rest."

" No, wretch accurs'd ! " relentless he replies
(Flames, as he spoke, shot flashing from his eyes),
" Not those who gave me breath should bid me spare,   435
Nor all the sacred prevalence of pray'r.
Could I myself the bloody banquet join !
No — to the dogs that carcase I resign.
Should Troy to bribe me bring forth all her store,
And, giving thousands, offer thousands more ;   440
Should Dardan Priam, and his weeping dame,
Drain their whole realm to buy one fun'ral flame ;
Their Hector on the pile they should not see,
Nor rob the vultures of one limb of thee."
    Then thus the chief his dying accents drew :   445
" Thy rage, implacable ! too well I knew :
The Furies that relentless breast have steel'd,
And curs'd thee with a heart that cannot yield.
Yet think, a day will come, when fate's decree
And angry gods shall wreak this wrong on thee ;   450
Phœbus and Paris shall avenge my fate,
And stretch thee here, before this Scæan gate."
    He ceas'd : the fates suppress'd his lab'ring breath,
And his eyes stiffen'd at the hand of death ;
To the dark realm the spirit wings its way   455
(The manly body left a load of clay),
And plaintive glides along the dreary coast,
A naked, wand'ring, melancholy ghost !
    Achilles, musing as he roll'd his eyes
O'er the dead hero, thus (unheard) replies :   460
" Die thou the first ! when Jove and heav'n ordain,
I follow thee."   He said, and stripp'd the slain.
Then, forcing backward from the gaping wound
The reeking jav'lin, cast it on the ground.
The thronging Greeks behold, with wond'ring eyes,   465
His manly beauty and superior size :

While some, ignobler, the great dead deface
With wounds ungen'rous, or with taunts disgrace.
" How chang'd that Hector ! who, like Jove, of late
Sent light'ning on our fleets and scatter'd fate ! "   470
    High o'er the slain the great Achilles stands,
Begirt with heroes and surrounding bands;
And thus aloud, while all the host attends :
" Princes and leaders ! countrymen and friends !
Since now at length the pow'rful will of heav'n   475
The dire destroyer to our arm has giv'n,
Is not Troy fall'n already ? Haste, ye pow'rs !
See if already their deserted tow'rs
Are left unmann'd ; or if they yet retain
The souls of heroes, their great Hector slain.   480
But what is Troy, or glory what to me ?
Or why reflects my mind on aught but thee,
Divine Patroclus ! Death has seal'd his eyes ;
Unwept, unhonour'd, uninterr'd he lies !
Can his dear image from my soul depart,   485
Long as the vital spirit moves my heart ?
If, in the melancholy shades below,
The flames of friends and lovers cease to glow,
Yet mine shall sacred last ; mine, undecay'd,
Burn on thro' death, and animate my shade.   490
Meanwhile, ye sons of Greece, in triumph bring
The corse of Hector, and your pæans sing.
Be this the song, slow moving tow'rd the shore,
' Hector is dead, and Ilion is no more.' "
    Then his fell soul a thought of vengeance bred   495
(Unworthy of himself, and of the dead) ;
The nervous ancles bor'd, his feet he bound
With thongs inserted thro' the double wound ;
These fix'd up high behind the rolling wain,
His graceful head was trail'd along the plain.   500

Proud on his car th' insulting victor stood,
And bore aloft his arms, distilling blood.
He smites the steeds; the rapid chariot flies;
The sudden clouds of circling dust arise.
Now lost is all that formidable air; 505
The face divine and long-descending hair
Purple the ground, and streak the sable sand;
Deform'd, dishonour'd, in his native land!
Giv'n to the rage of an insulting throng!
And, in his parents' sight, now dragg'd along! 510
    The mother first beheld with sad survey;
She rent her tresses, venerably grey,
And cast far off the regal veils away.
With piercing shrieks his bitter fate she moans,
While the sad father answers groans with groans; 515
Tears after tears his mournful cheeks o'erflow,
And the whole city wears one face of woe:
No less than if the rage of hostile fires,
From her foundations curling to her spires,
O'er the proud citadel at length should rise, 520
And the last blaze send Ilion to the skies.
The wretched monarch of the falling state,
Distracted, presses to the Dardan gate:
Scarce the whole people stop his desp'rate course,
While strong affliction gives the feeble force: 525
Grief tears his heart, and drives him to and fro,
In all the raging impotence of woe.
At length he roll'd in dust, and thus begun,
Imploring all, and naming one by one:
"Ah! let me, let me go where sorrow calls; 530
I, only I, will issue from your walls
(Guide or companion, friends! I ask ye none),
And bow before the murd'rer of my son;
My grief perhaps his pity may engage;

Perhaps at least he may respect my age.   535
He has a father, too; a man like me;
One not exempt from age and misery
(Vig'rous no more, as when his young embrace
Begot this pest of me and all my race).
How many valiant sons, in early bloom,   540
Has that curs'd hand sent headlong to the tomb!
Thee, Hector! last; thy loss (divinely brave!)
Sinks my sad soul with sorrow to the grave.
Oh had thy gentle spirit pass'd in peace,
The son expiring in the sire's embrace,   545
While both thy parents wept thy fatal hour,
And, bending o'er thee, mix'd the tender show'r!
Some comfort that had been, some sad relief,
To melt in full satiety of grief!"
    Thus wail'd the father, grov'ling on the ground,   550
And all the eyes of Ilion stream'd around.
    Amidst her matrons Hecuba appears
(A mourning princess, and a train in tears):
"Ah! why has heav'n prolong'd this hated breath,
Patient of horrours, to behold thy death?   555
O Hector! late thy parents' pride and joy,
The boast of nations! the defence of Troy!
To whom her safety and her fame she ow'd,
Her chief, her hero, and almost her god!
O fatal change! become in one sad day   560
A senseless corse! inanimated clay!"
    But not as yet the fatal news had spread
To fair Andromache, of Hector dead;
As yet no messenger had told his fate,
Nor ev'n his stay without the Scæan gate.   565
Far in the close recesses of the dome,
Pensive she plied the melancholy loom;
A growing work employ'd her secret hours,

Confus'dly gay with intermingled flow'rs.
Her fair-hair'd handmaids heat the brazen urn,   570
The bath preparing for her lord's return :
In vain : alas ! her lord returns no more !
Unbath'd he lies, and bleeds along the shore !
Now from the walls the clamours reach her ear,
And all her members shake with sudden fear ;   575
Forth from her iv'ry hand the shuttle falls,
As thus, astonish'd, to her maids she calls :
    " Ah, follow me ! " she cried ; " what plaintive noise
Invades my ear? 'T is sure my mother's voice.
My falt'ring knees their trembling frame desert,   580
A pulse unusual flutters at my heart.
Some strange disaster, some reverse of fate
(Ye gods avert it !) threats the Trojan state.
Far be the omen which my thoughts suggest !
But much I fear my Hector's dauntless breast   585
Confronts Achilles ; chas'd along the plain,
Shut from our walls ! I fear, I fear him slain !
Safe in the crowd he ever scorn'd to wait,
And sought for glory in the jaws of fate :
Perhaps that noble heat has cost his breath,   590
Now quench'd for ever in the arms of death."
    She spoke ; and, furious, with distracted pace,
Fears in her heart, and anguish in her face,
Flies thro' the dome (the maids her step pursue),
And mounts the walls, and sends around her view.   595
Too soon her eyes the killing object found,
The godlike Hector dragg'd along the ground.
A sudden darkness shades her swimming eyes :
She faints, she falls ; her breath, her colour flies.
Her hair's fair ornaments, the braids that bound,   600
The net that held them, and the wreath that crown'd,
The veil and diadem, flew far away

(The gift of Venus on her bridal day).
Around, a train of weeping sisters stands,
To raise her sinking with assistant hands.   605
Scarce from the verge of death recall'd, again
She faints, or but recovers to complain :

   "O wretched husband of a wretched wife!
Born with one fate, to one unhappy life !
For sure one star its baneful beam display'd   610
On Priam's roof and Hippoplacia's shade.
From diff'rent parents, diff'rent climes, we came,
At diff'rent periods, yet our fate the same !
Why was my birth to great Eëtion ow'd,
And why was all that tender care bestow'd?   615
Would I had never been !— O thou, the ghost
Of my dead husband! miserably lost !
Thou to the dismal realms for ever gone!
And I abandon'd, desolate, alone!
An only child, once comfort of my pains,   620
Sad product now of hapless love, remains !
No more to smile upon his sire ! no friend
To help him now ! no father to defend !
For should he 'scape the sword, the common doom,
What wrongs attend him, and what griefs to come !   625
Ev'n from his own paternal roof expell'd,
Some stranger ploughs his patrimonial field.
The day that to the shades the father sends,
Robs the sad orphan of his father's friends :
He, wretched outcast of mankind ! appears   630
For ever sad, for ever bath'd in tears ;
Amongst the happy, unregarded he
Hangs on the robe or trembles at the knee ;
While those his father's former bounty fed,
Nor reach the goblet, nor divide the bread :   635
The kindest but his present wants allay,

To leave him wretched the succeeding day.
Frugal compassion ! Heedless, they who boast
Both parents still, nor feel what he has lost,
Shall cry, 'Begone ! thy father feasts not here':   640
The wretch obeys, retiring with a tear.
Thus wretched, thus retiring all in tears,
To my sad soul Astyanax appears !
Forc'd by repeated insults to return,
And to his widow'd mother vainly mourn,   645
He who, with tender delicacy bred,
With princes sported, and on dainties fed,
And, when still ev'ning gave him up to rest,
Sunk soft in down upon the nurse's breast,
Must —ah! what must he not?   Whom Ilion calls   650
Astyanax, from her well-guarded walls,
Is now that name no more, unhappy boy !
Since now no more the father guards his Troy.
But thou, my Hector ! liest expos'd in air,
Far from thy parents' and thy consort's care,   655
Whose hand in vain, directed by her love,
The martial scarf and robe of triumph wove.
Now to devouring flames be these a prey,
Useless to thee, from this accursed day !
Yet let the sacrifice at least be paid,   660
An honour to the living, not the dead !"
    So spake the mournful dame : her matrons hear,
Sigh back her sighs, and answer tear with tear.

BOOK XXIV.

THE REDEMPTION OF THE BODY OF HECTOR.

Now from the finish'd games the Grecian band
Seek their black ships, and clear the crowded strand:
All stretch'd at ease the genial banquet share,
And pleasing slumbers quiet all their care.
Not so Achilles: he, to grief resign'd,   5
His friend's dear image present to his mind,
Takes his sad couch, more unobserv'd to weep,
Nor tastes the gifts of all-composing sleep;
Restless he roll'd around his weary bed,
And all his soul on his Patroclus fed: 10
The form so pleasing, and the heart so kind,
That youthful vigour, and that manly mind,
What toils they shar'd, what martial works they wrought,
What seas they measur'd, and what fields they fought;
All pass'd before him in rememb'rance dear,   15
Thought follows thought, and tear succeeds to tear.
And now supine, now prone, the hero lay,
Now shifts his side, impatient for the day;
Then starting up, disconsolate he goes
Wide on the lonely beach to vent his woes.   20
There as the solitary mourner raves,
The ruddy morning rises o'er the waves:
Soon as it rose, his furious steeds he join'd;
The chariot flies, and Hector trails behind.
And thrice, Patroclus! round thy monument   25
Was Hector dragg'd, then hurried to the tent.

There sleep at last o'ercomes the hero's eyes ;
While foul in dust th' unhonour'd carcase lies,
But not deserted by the pitying skies.
For Phœbus watch'd it with superior care, 30
Preserv'd from gaping wounds, and tainting air ;
And, ignominious as it swept the field,
Spread o'er the sacred corse his golden shield.
All heav'n was mov'd, and Hermes will'd to go
By stealth to snatch him from th' insulting foe : 35
But Neptune this, and Pallas this denies,
And th' unrelenting empress of the skies :
E'er since that day implacable to Troy,
What time young Paris, simple shepherd boy,
Won by destructive lust (reward obscene), 40
Their charms rejected for the Cyprian queen.
But when the tenth celestial morning broke,
To heav'n assembled, thus Apollo spoke:
   " Unpitying pow'rs ! how oft each holy fane
Has Hector ting'd with blood of victims slain ! 45
And can ye still his cold remains pursue ?
Still grudge his body to the Trojans' view ?
Deny to consort, mother, son, and sire,
The last sad honours of a fun'ral fire ?
Is then the dire Achilles all your care ? 50
That iron heart, inflexibly severe ;
A lion, not a man, who slaughters wide
In strength of rage and impotence of pride,
Who hastes to murder with a savage joy,
Invades around, and breathes but to destroy. 55
Shame is not of his soul ; nor understood
The greatest evil and the greatest good.
Still for one loss he rages unresign'd,
Repugnant to the lot of all mankind ;
To lose a friend, a brother, or a son, 60

Heav'n dooms each mortal, and its will is done:
Awhile they sorrow, then dismiss their care;
Fate gives the wound, and man is born to bear.
But this insatiate the commission giv'n
By fate exceeds, and tempts the wrath of heav'n: 65
Lo how his rage dishonest drags along
Hector's dead earth, insensible of wrong!
Brave tho' he be, yet by no reason aw'd,
He violates the laws of man and God!"

  "If equal honours by the partial skies   70
Are doom'd both heroes," Juno thus replies,
"If Thetis' son must no distinction know,
Then hear, ye gods! the patron of the bow.
But Hector only boasts a mortal claim,
His birth deriving from a mortal dame: 75
Achilles, of your own æthereal race,
Springs from a goddess, by a man's embrace
(A goddess by ourself to Peleus giv'n,
A man divine, and chosen friend of heav'n):
To grace those nuptials, from the bright abode   80
Yourselves were present; where this minstrel-god
(Well-pleas'd to share the feast) amid the quire
Stood proud to hymn, and tune his youthful lyre."

  Then thus the Thund'rer checks th' imperial dame:
"Let not thy wrath the court of heav'n inflame;   85
Their merits nor their honours are the same.
But mine, and ev'ry god's peculiar grace
Hector deserves, of all the Trojan race:
Still on our shrines his grateful off'rings lay
(The only honours men to gods can pay),   90
Nor ever from our smoking altar ceas'd
The pure libation, and the holy feast.
Howe'er, by stealth to snatch the corse away,
We will not: Thetis guards it night and day.

But haste, and summon to our courts above 95
The azure queen : let her persuasion move
Her furious son from Priam to receive
The proffer'd ransom, and the corse to leave."
He added not : and Iris from the skies,
Swift as a whirlwind, on the message flies ; 100
Meteorous the face of ocean sweeps,
Refulgent gliding o'er the sable deeps.
Between where Samos wide his forests spreads,
And rocky Imbrus lifts its pointed heads,
Down plung'd the maid (the parted waves resound) ; 105
She plung'd, and instant shot the dark profound.
As, bearing death in the fallacious bait,
From the bent angle sinks the leaden weight ;
So pass'd the goddess thro' the closing wave,
Where Thetis sorrow'd in her secret cave : 110
There plac'd amidst her melancholy train
(The blue-hair'd sisters of the sacred main)
Pensive she sat, revolving fates to come,
And wept her godlike son's approaching doom.
Then thus the goddess of the painted bow : 115
" Arise, O Thetis ! from thy seats below ;
'T is Jove that calls." " And why," the dame replies,
" Calls Jove his Thetis to the hated skies ?
Sad object as I am for heav'nly sight !
Ah ! may my sorrows ever shun the light ! 120
Howe'er, be heav'n's almighty sire obey'd."
She spake, and veil'd her head in sable shade,
Which, flowing long, her graceful person clad ;
And forth she pac'd majestically sad.
Then through the world of waters they repair 125
(The way fair Iris led) to upper air.
The deeps dividing, o'er the coast they rise,
And touch with momentary flight the skies.

There in the light'ning's blaze the sire they found,
And all the gods in shining synod round. 130
Thetis approach'd with anguish in her face
(Minerva rising gave the mourner place),
Ev'n Juno sought her sorrows to console,
And offer'd from her hand the nectar-bowl:
She tasted, and resign'd it : then began 135
The sacred sire of gods and mortal man:
    "Thou com'st, fair Thetis, but with grief o'ercast,
Maternal sorrows, long, ah long to last !
Suffice, we know and we partake thy cares :
But yield to fate, and hear what Jove declares. 140
Nine days are past, since all the court above
In Hector's cause have mov'd the ear of Jove ;
'Twas voted, Hermes from his godlike foe
By stealth should bear him, but we will'd not so :
We will, thy son himself the corse restore, 145
And to his conquest add this glory more.
Then hie thee to him, and our mandate bear ;
Tell him he tempts the wrath of heav'n too far :
Nor let him more (our anger if he dread)
Vent his sad vengeance on the sacred dead : 150
But yield to ransom and the father's pray'r.
The mournful father Iris shall prepare,
With gifts to sue, and offer to his hands
Whate'er his honour asks or heart demands."
    His word the silver-footed queen attends, 155
And from Olympus' snowy tops descends.
Arriv'd, she heard the voice of loud lament,
And echoing groans that shook the lofty tent.
His friends prepare the victim, and dispose
Repast unheeded, while he vents his woes. 160
The goddess seats her by her pensive son ;
She press'd his hand, and tender thus begun :

" How long, unhappy ! shall thy sorrows flow,
And thy heart waste with life-consuming woe,
Mindless of food, or love, whose pleasing reign   165
Soothes weary life, and softens human pain ?
Oh snatch the moments yet within thy pow'r ;
Not long to live, indulge the am'rous hour !
Lo ! Jove himself (for Jove's command I bear)
Forbids to tempt the wrath of heav'n too far.   170
No longer then (his fury if thou dread)
Detain the relics of great Hector dead ;
Nor vent on senseless earth thy vengeance vain,
But yield to ransom, and restore the slain."

   To whom Achilles : " Be the ransom giv'n,   175
And we submit, since such the will of heav'n."

   While thus they commun'd, from th' Olympian bow'rs
Jove orders Iris to the Trojan tow'rs :
" Haste, winged goddess, to the sacred town,
And urge her monarch to redeem his son ;   180
Alone the Ilian ramparts let him leave,
And bear what stern Achilles may receive :
Alone, for so we will : no Trojan near,
Except, to place the dead with decent care,
Some aged herald, who, with gentle hand,   185
May the slow mules and fun'ral car command.
Nor let him death, nor let him danger dread,
Safe thro' the foe by our protection led :
Him Hermes to Achilles shall convey,
Guard of his life, and partner of his way.   190
Fierce as he is, Achilles' self shall spare
His age, nor touch one venerable hair :
Some thought there must be in a soul so brave,
Some sense of duty, some desire to save."

   Then down her bow the winged Iris drives,   195
And swift at Priam's mournful court arrives :

Where the sad sons beside their father's throne
Sate bathed in tears, and answer'd groan with groan.
And all amidst them lay the hoary sire
(Sad scene of woe!), his face his wrapp'd attire   200
Conceal'd from sight; with frantic hands he spread
A show'r of ashes o'er his neck and head.
From room to room his pensive daughters roam:
Whose shrieks and clamours fill the vaulted dome;
Mindful of those who, late their pride and joy,   205
Lie pale and breathless round the fields of Troy!
Before the king Jove's messenger appears,
And thus in whispers greets his trembling ears:
    "Fear not, O father! no ill news I bear;
From Jove I come, Jove makes thee still his care;   210
For Hector's sake these walls he bids thee leave,
And bear what stern Achilles may receive:
Alone, for so he wills: no Trojan near,
Except, to place the dead with decent care,
Some aged herald, who, with gentle hand,   215
May the slow mules and fun'ral car command.
Nor shalt thou death, nor shalt thou danger dread,
Safe thro' the foe by his protection led:
Thee Hermes to Pelides shall convey,
Guard of thy life, and partner of thy way.   220
Fierce as he is, Achilles' self shall spare
Thy age, nor touch one venerable hair:
Some thought there must be in a soul so brave,
Some sense of duty, some desire to save."
    She spoke, and vanish'd.   Priam bids prepare   225
His gentle mules, and harness to the car;
There, for the gifts, a polish'd casket lay:
His pious sons the king's commands obey.
Then passed the monarch to his bridal-room,
Where cedar-beams the lofty roofs perfume,   230

And where the treasures of his empire lay;
Then call'd his queen, and thus began to say:
    "Unhappy consort of a king distress'd!
Partake the troubles of thy husband's breast:
I saw descend the messenger of Jove,   235
Who bids me try Achilles' mind to move,
Forsake these ramparts, and with gifts obtain
The corse of Hector, at yon navy slain.
Tell me thy thought: my heart impels to go
Thro' hostile camps, and bears me to the foe."   240
    The hoary monarch thus: her piercing cries
Sad Hecuba renews, and then replies:
"Ah! whither wanders thy distemper'd mind;
And where the prudence now that aw'd mankind,
Thro' Phrygia once and foreign regions known?   245
Now all confus'd, distracted, overthrown!
Singly to pass thro' hosts of foes! to face
(Oh heart of steel!) the murd'rer of thy race!
To view that deathful eye, and wander o'er
Those hands, yet red with Hector's noble gore!   250
Alas! my lord! he knows not how to spare,
And what his mercy, thy slain sons declare;
So brave! so many fall'n!   To calm his rage
Vain were thy dignity, and vain thy age.
No — pent in this sad palace, let us give   255
To grief the wretched days we have to live.
Still, still for Hector let our sorrows flow,
Born to his own and to his parents' woe!
Doom'd from the hour his luckless life begun,
To dogs, to vultures, and to Peleus' son!   260
Oh! in his dearest blood might I allay
My rage, and these barbarities repay!
For ah! could Hector merit thus, whose breath
Expir'd not meanly in unactive death?

He pour'd his latest blood in manly fight,   265
And fell a hero in his country's right."
    "Seek not to stay me, nor my soul affright
With words of omen, like a bird of night,"
Replied unmov'd the venerable man :
"'T is heav'n commands me, and you urge in vain.   270
Had any mortal voice th' injunction laid,
Nor augur, priest, nor seer had been obey'd.
A present goddess brought the high command:
I saw, I heard her, and the word shall stand.
I go, ye gods ! obedient to your call :   275
If in yon camp your pow'rs have doom'd my fall,
Content : by the same hand let me expire !
Add to the slaughter'd son the wretched sire !
One cold embrace at least may be allow'd,
And my last tears flow mingled with his blood !"   280
    Forth from his open'd stores, this said, he drew
Twelve costly carpets of refulgent hue ;
As many vests, as many mantles told,
And twelve fair veils, and garments stiff with gold ;
Two tripods next, and twice two charges shine,   285
With ten pure talents from the richest mine ;
And last a large, well-labour'd bowl had place
(The pledge of treaties once with friendly Thrace):
Seem'd all too mean the stores he could employ,
For one last look to buy him back to Troy !   290
    Lo ! the sad father, frantic with his pain,
Around him furious drives his menial train :
In vain each slave with duteous care attends,
Each office hurts him, and each face offends.
"What make ye here, officious crowds !" he cries ;   295
" Hence, nor obtrude your anguish on my eyes.
Have ye no griefs at home, to fix ye there ?
Am I the only object of despair ?

Am I become my people's common show,
Set up by Jove your spectacle of woe?   300
No, you must feel him too : yourselves must fall ;
The same stern god to ruin gives you all :
Nor is great Hector lost by me alone ;
Your sole defence, your guardian pow'r, is gone !
I see your blood the fields of Phrygia drown ;   305
I see the ruins of your smoking town !
Oh send me, gods, ere that sad day shall come,
A willing ghost to Pluto's dreary dome !"
    He said, and feebly drives his friends away :
The sorrowing friends his frantic rage obey.   310
Next on his sons his erring fury falls,
Polites, Paris, Agathon, he calls ;
His threats Deïphobus and Dius hear,
Hippothoüs, Pammon, Helenus the seer,
And gen'rous Antiphon ; for yet these nine   315
Surviv'd, sad relics of his num'rous line.
    " Inglorious sons of an unhappy sire !
Why did not all in Hector's cause expire ?
Wretch that I am ! my bravest offspring slain,
You, the disgrace of Priam's house, remain !   320
Mestor the brave, renown'd in ranks of war,
With Troilus, dreadful on his rushing car,
And last great Hector, more than man divine,
For sure he seem'd not of terrestrial line !
All those relentless Mars untimely slew,   325
And left me these, a soft and servile crew,
Whose days the feast and wanton dance employ,
Gluttons and flatt'rers, the contempt of Troy !
Why teach ye not my rapid wheels to run,
And speed my journey to redeem my son ?"   330
    The sons their father's wretched age revere,
Forgive his anger, and produce the car.

High on the seat the cabinet they bind:
The new-made car with solid beauty shin'd:
Box was the yoke, emboss'd with costly pains,   335
And hung with ringlets to receive the reins:
Nine cubits long, the traces swept the ground;
These to the chariot's polish'd pole they bound,
Then fix'd a ring the running reins to guide,
And, close beneath, the gather'd ends were tied.   340
Next with the gifts (the price of Hector slain)
The sad attendants load the groaning wain:
Last to the yoke the well-match'd mules they bring
(The gift of Mysia to the Trojan king).
But the fair horses, long his darling care,   345
Himself receiv'd, and harness'd to his car:
Griev'd as he was, he not this task denied;
The hoary herald help'd him at his side.
While careful these the gentle coursers join'd,
Sad Hecuba approach'd with anxious mind;   350
A golden bowl, that foam'd with fragrant wine
(Libation destin'd to the pow'r divine),
Held in her right, before the steeds she stands,
And thus consigns it to the monarch's hands:

   "Take this, and pour to Jove; that, safe from harms,   355
His grace restore thee to our roof and arms.
Since, victor of thy fears, and slighting mine,
Heav'n or thy soul inspire this bold design,
Pray to that god who, high on Ida's brow,
Surveys thy desolated realms below,   360
His winged messenger to send from high,
And lead the way with heav'nly augury:
Let the strong sov'reign of the plumy race
Tow'r on the right of yon æthereal space.
That sign beheld, and strengthen'd from above,   365
Boldly pursue the journey mark'd by Jove;

But if the god his augury denies,
Suppress thy impulse, nor reject advice."
   "'Tis just," said Priam, "to the sire above
To raise our hands ; for who so good as Jove?" 370
   He spoke, and bade th' attendant handmaid bring
The purest water of the living spring
(Her ready hands the ewer and bason held) ;
Then took the golden cup his queen had fill'd ;
On the mid pavement pours the rosy wine, 375
Uplifts his eyes, and calls the pow'r divine :
   " O first and greatest ! heav'n's imperial lord !
On lofty Ida's holy hill ador'd !
To stern Achilles now direct my ways,
And teach him mercy when a father prays. 380
If such thy will, dispatch from yonder sky
Thy sacred bird, celestial augury !
Let the strong sov'reign of the plumy race
Tow'r on the right of yon æthereal space :
So shall thy suppliant, strengthen'd from above, 385
Fearless pursue the journey mark'd by Jove."
   Jove heard his pray'r, and from the throne on high
Dispatch'd his bird, celestial augury !
The swift-wing'd chaser of the feather'd game,
And known to gods by Percnos' lofty name. 390
Wide as appears some palace-gate display'd,
So broad his pinions stretch'd their ample shade,
As, stooping dexter with resounding wings,
Th' imperial bird descends in airy rings.
A dawn of joy in ev'ry face appears ; 395
The mourning matron dries her tim'rous tears.
Swift on his car th' impatient monarch sprung ;
The brazen portal in his passage rung.
The mules preceding draw the loaded wain,
Charg'd with the gifts ; Idæus holds the rein : 400

The king himself his gentle steeds controls,
And thro' surrounding friends the chariot rolls:
On his slow wheels the following people wait,
Mourn at each step, and give him up to fate;
With hands uplifted, eye him as he pass'd,   405
And gaze upon him as they gaz'd their last.
　　Now forward fares the father on his way,
Thro' the lone fields, and back to Ilion they.
Great Jove beheld him as he cross'd the plain,
And felt the woes of miserable man.   410
Then thus to Hermes: "Thou, whose constant cares
Still succour mortals, and attend their pray'rs!
Behold an object to thy charge consign'd;
If ever pity touch'd thee for mankind,
Go, guard the sire; th' observing foe prevent,   415
And safe conduct him to Achilles' tent."
　　The god obeys, his golden pinions binds,
And mounts incumbent on the wings of winds,
That high thro' fields of air his flight sustain,
O'er the wide earth, and o'er the boundless main: 420
Then grasps the wand that causes sleep to fly,
Or in soft slumbers seals the wakeful eye:
Thus arm'd, swift Hermes steers his airy way,
And stoops on Hellespont's resounding sea.
A beauteous youth, majestic and divine,   425
He seem'd; fair offspring of some princely line!
Now twilight veil'd the glaring face of day,
And clad the dusky fields in sober gray;
What time the herald and the hoary king,
Their chariot stopping at the silver spring,   430
That circling Ilus' ancient marble flows,
Allow'd their mules and steeds a short repose.
Thro' the dim shade the herald first espies
A man's approach, and thus to Priam cries:

" I mark some foe's advance : O king ! beware ;   435
This hard adventure claims thy utmost care ;
For much I fear destruction hovers nigh :
Our state asks counsel. Is it best to fly?
Or, old and helpless, at his feet to fall
(Two wretched suppliants), and for mercy call? "   440
    Th' afflicted monarch shiver'd with despair ;
Pale grew his face, and upright stood his hair ;
Sunk was his heart ; his colour went and came ;
A sudden trembling shook his aged frame :
When Hermes, greeting, touch'd his royal hand,   445
And, gentle, thus accosts with kind demand :
    " Say whither, father ! when each mortal sight
Is seal'd in sleep, thou wander'st thro' the night.
Why roam thy mules and steeds the plains along,
Thro' Grecian foes, so num'rous and so strong ?   450
What could'st thou hope, should these thy treasures view,
These, who with endless hate thy race pursue ?
For what defence, alas ! could'st thou provide,
Thyself not young, a weak old man thy guide ?
Yet suffer not thy soul to sink with dread ;   455
From me no harm shall touch thy rev'rend head :
From Greece I 'll guard thee too ; for in those lines
The living image of my father shines."
    " Thy words, that speak benevolence of mind,
Are true, my son ! " the godlike sire rejoin'd :   460
" Great are my hazards ; but the gods survey
My steps, and send thee guardian of my way.
Hail ! and be blest ! for scarce of mortal kind
Appear thy form, thy feature, and thy mind."
    " Nor true are all thy words, nor erring wide,"   465
The sacred messenger of heav'n replied :
" But say, convey'st thou thro' the lonely plains
What yet most precious of thy store remains,

To lodge in safety with some friendly hand,
Prepar'd perchance to leave thy native land?   470
Or fly'st thou now?   What hopes can Troy retain,
Thy matchless son, her guard and glory, slain?"
    The king, alarm'd : " Say what, and whence thou art,
Who search the sorrows of a parent's heart,
And know so well how godlike Hector died."   475
Thus Priam spoke, and Hermes thus replied :
    " You tempt me, father, and with pity touch :
On this sad subject you enquire too much.
Oft have these eyes the godlike Hector view'd
In glorious fight, with Grecian blood embru'd :   480
I saw him when, like Jove, his flames he toss'd
On thousand ships, and wither'd half a host :
I saw, but help'd not; stern Achilles' ire
Forbade assistance, and enjoy'd the fire.
For him I serve, of Myrmidonian race ;   485
One ship convey'd us from our native place ;
Polyctor is my sire, an honour'd name,
Old, like thyself, and not unknown to fame ;
Of sev'n his sons, by whom the lot was cast
To serve our prince, it fell on me, the last.   490
To watch this quarter my adventure falls ;
For with the morn the Greeks attack your walls ;
Sleepless they sit, impatient to engage,
And scarce their rulers check their martial rage."
    " If then thou art of stern Pelides' train "   495
(The mournful monarch thus rejoin'd again),
" Ah, tell me truly, where, oh ! where are laid
My son's dear relics ? what befalls him dead ?
Have dogs dismember'd on the naked plains,
Or yet unmangled rest his cold remains ? "   500
    " O favour'd of the skies ! " thus answer'd then
The pow'r that mediates between gods and men,

" Nor dogs nor vultures have thy Hector rent,
But whole he lies, neglected in the tent :
This the twelfth ev'ning since he rested there, 505
Untouch'd by worms, untainted by the air.
Still as Aurora's ruddy beam is spread,
Round his friend's tomb Achilles drags the dead ;
Yet undisfigur'd, or in limb or face,
All fresh he lies, with ev'ry living grace, 510
Majestical in death ! No stains are found
O'er all the corse, and clos'd is ev'ry wound ;
Tho' many a wound they gave. Some heav'nly care,
Some hand divine, preserves him ever fair :
Or all the host of heav'n, to whom he led 515
A life so grateful, still regard him dead."
   Thus spoke to Priam the celestial guide,
And joyful thus the royal sire replied :
" Bless'd is the man who pays the gods above
The constant tribute of respect and love ! 520
Those who inhabit the Olympian bow'r
My son forgot not, in exalted pow'r ;
And heav'n, that ev'ry virtue bears in mind,
Ev'n to the ashes of the just is kind.
But thou, O gen'rous youth ! this goblet take, 525
A pledge of gratitude for Hector's sake ;
And while the fav'ring gods our steps survey,
Safe to Pelides' tent conduct my way."
   To whom the latent god : " O king, forbear
To tempt my youth, for apt is youth to err : 530
But can I, absent from my prince's sight,
Take gifts in secret, that must shun the light ?
What from our master's int'rest thus we draw
Is but a licens'd theft that 'scapes the law.
Respecting him, my soul abjures th' offence ; 535
And, as the crime, I dread the consequence.

Thee, far as Argos, pleas'd I could convey;
Guard of thy life, and partner of thy way:
On thee attend, thy safety to maintain,
O'er pathless forests, or the roaring main."   540
    He said, then took the chariot at a bound,
And snatch'd the reins, and whirl'd the lash around:
Before th' inspiring god that urg'd them on
The coursers fly, with spirit not their own.
And now they reach'd the naval walls, and found   545
The guards repasting, while the bowls go round:
On these the virtue of his wand he tries,
And pours deep slumber on their watchful eyes:
Then heav'd the massy gates, remov'd the bars,
And o'er the trenches led the rolling cars.   550
Unseen, thro' all the hostile camp they went,
And now approach'd Pelides' lofty tent.
Of fir the roof was rais'd, and cover'd o'er
With reeds collected from the marshy shore;
And, fenc'd with palisades, a hall of state   555
(The work of soldiers), where the hero sate.
Large was the door, whose well-compacted strength
A solid pine-tree barr'd of wond'rous length;
Scarce three strong Greeks could lift its mighty weight,
But great Achilles singly clos'd the gate.   560
This Hermes (such the pow'r of gods) set wide;
Then swift alighted the celestial guide,
And thus, reveal'd: "Hear, prince! and understand
Thou ow'st thy guidance to no mortal hand;
Hermes I am, descended from above,   565
The king of arts, the messenger of Jove.
Farewell: to shun Achilles' sight I fly;
Uncommon are such favours of the sky,
Nor stand confess'd to frail mortality.
Now fearless enter, and prefer thy pray'rs;   570

Adjure him by his father's silver hairs,
His son, his mother! urge him to bestow
Whatever pity that stern heart can know."
   Thus having said, he vanish'd from his eyes,
And in a moment shot into the skies: 575
The king, confirm'd from heav'n, alighted there,
And left his aged herald on the car.
With solemn pace thro' various rooms he went,
And found Achilles in his inner tent:
There sat the hero; Alcimus the brave,   580
And great Automedon, attendance gave;
These served his person at the royal feast;
Around, at awful distance, stood the rest.
   Unseen by these, the king his entry made;
And, prostrate now before Achilles laid,   585
Sudden (a venerable sight!) appears;
Embrac'd his knees, and bath'd his hands in tears;
Those direful hands his kisses press'd, embru'd
Ev'n with the best, the dearest of his blood!
   As when a wretch (who, conscious of his crime,   590
Pursu'd for murder, flies his native clime)
Just gains some frontier, breathless, pale, amaz'd!
All gaze, all wonder: thus Achilles gaz'd:
Thus stood th' attendants stupid with surprise:
All mute, yet seem'd to question with their eyes: 595
Each look'd on other, none the silence broke,
Till thus at last the kingly suppliant spoke:
   "Ah think, thou favour'd of the pow'rs divine!
Think of thy father's age, and pity mine!
In me, that father's rev'rend image trace,   600
Those silver hairs, that venerable face;
His trembling limbs, his helpless person, see!
In all my equal, but in misery!
Yet now, perhaps, some turn of human fate

Expels him helpless from his peaceful state;   605
Think, from some pow'rful foe thou see'st him fly,
And beg protection with a feeble cry.
Yet still one comfort in his soul may rise;
He hears his son still lives to glad his eyes;
And, hearing, still may hope a better day   610
May send him thee, to chase that foe away.
No comfort to my griefs, no hopes remain,
The best, the bravest of my sons are slain!
Yet what a race! ere Greece to Ilion came,
The pledge of many a lov'd and loving dame!   615
Nineteen one mother bore — dead, all are dead!
How oft, alas! has wretched Priam bled!
Still one was left, their loss to recompense;
His father's hope, his country's last defence.
Him too thy rage has slain! beneath thy steel,   620
Unhappy, in his country's cause, he fell!
For him thro' hostile camps I bent my way,
For him thus prostrate at thy feet I lay;
Large gifts, proportion'd to thy wrath, I bear:
Oh, hear the wretched, and the gods revere!   625
Think of thy father, and this face behold!
See him in me, as helpless and as old;
Tho' not so wretched: there he yields to me,
The first of men in sov'reign misery:
Thus forc'd to kneel, thus grov'ling to embrace   630
The scourge and ruin of my realm and race:
Suppliant my children's murd'rer to implore,
And kiss those hands yet reeking with their gore!"
    These words soft pity in the chief inspire,
Touch'd with the dear rememb'rance of his sire.   635
Then with his hand (as prostrate still he lay)
The old man's cheek he gently turn'd away.
Now each by turns indulg'd the gush of woe;

And now the mingled tides together flow :
This low on earth, that gently bending o'er,   640
A father one, and one a son deplore :
But great Achilles diff'rent passions rend,
And now his sire he mourns, and now his friend.
Th' infectious softness thro' the heroes ran ;
One universal solemn show'r began ;   645
They bore as heroes, but they felt as man.
   Satiate at length with unavailing woes,
From the high throne divine Achilles rose ;
The rev'rend monarch by the hand he rais'd ;
On his white beard and form majestic gaz'd,   650
Not unrelenting : then serene began
With words to soothe the miserable man :
   "Alas ! what weight of anguish hast thou known,
Unhappy prince ! thus guardless and alone
To pass thro' foes, and thus undaunted face   655
The man whose fury has destroy'd thy race !
Heav'n sure has arm'd thee with a heart of steel,
A strength proportion'd to the woes you feel.
Rise then : let reason mitigate our care :
To mourn avails not : man is born to bear.   660
Such is, alas ! the gods' severe decree ;
They, only they are blest, and only free.
Two urns by Jove's high throne have ever stood,
The source of evil one, and one of good ;
From thence the cup of mortal man he fills,   665
Blessings to these, to those distributes ills ;
To most he mingles both : the wretch decreed
To taste the bad unmix'd, is curs'd indeed :
Pursu'd by wrongs, by meagre famine driv'n,
He wanders, outcast both of earth and heav'n.   670
The happiest taste not happiness sincere,
But find the cordial draught is dash'd with care.

Who more than Peleus shone in wealth and pow'r?
What stars concurring bless'd his natal hour!
A realm, a goddess, to his wishes giv'n,   675
Grac'd by the gods with all the gifts of heav'n! ·
One evil, yet, o'ertakes his latest day;
No race succeeding to imperial sway:
An only son! and he (alas!) ordain'd
To fall untimely in a foreign land!   680
See him, in Troy, the pious care decline
Of his weak age, to live the curse of thine!
Thou too, old man, hast happier days beheld;
In riches once, in children once excell'd;
Extended Phrygia own'd thy ample reign,   685
And all fair Lesbos' blissful seats contain,
And all wide Hellespont's unmeasur'd main.
But since the god his hand has pleas'd to turn,
And fill thy measure from his bitter urn,
What sees the sun but hapless heroes' falls?   690
War and the blood of men surround thy walls!
What must be, must be.   Bear thy lot, nor shed
These unavailing sorrows o'er the dead;
Thou canst not call him from the Stygian shore,
But thou, alas! may'st live to suffer more!"   695
    To whom the king: "O favour'd of the skies!
Here let me grow to earth! since Hector lies
On the bare beach, depriv'd of obsequies.
Oh, give me Hector! to my eyes restore
His corse, and take the gifts: I ask no more!   700
Thou, as thou may'st, these boundless stores enjoy;
Safe may'st thou sail, and turn thy wrath from Troy;
So shall thy pity and forbearance give
A weak old man to see the light and live!"
    "Move me no more," Achilles thus replies,   705
While kindling anger sparkled in his eyes,

" Nor seek by tears my steady soul to bend.
To yield thy Hector I myself intend :
For know, from Jove my goddess-mother came
(Old Ocean's daughter, silver-footed dame) ;   710
Nor com'st thou but by heav'n ; nor com'st alone ;
Some god impels with courage not thy own :
No human hand the weighty gates unbarr'd,
Nor could the boldest of our youth have dar'd
To pass our out-works, or elude the guard.   715
Cease ; lest, neglectful of high Jove's command,
I show thee, king ! thou tread'st on hostile land ;
Release my knees, thy suppliant arts give o'er,
And shake the purpose of my soul no more."
 The sire obey'd him, trembling and o'eraw'd.   720
Achilles, like a lion, rush'd abroad ;
Automedon and Alcimus attend,
Whom most he honour'd since he lost his friend ;
These to unyoke the mules and horses went,
And led the hoary herald to the tent :   725
Next, heap'd on high, the num'rous presents bear
(Great Hector's ransom) from the polish'd car.
Two splendid mantles, and a carpet spread,
They leave, to cover and inwrap the dead :
Then call the handmaids, with assistant toil   730
To wash the body, and anoint with oil,
Apart from Priam ; lest th' unhappy sire,
Provok'd to passion, once more rouse to ire
The stern Pelides ; and nor sacred age
Nor Jove's command should check the rising rage.   735
This done, the garments o'er the corse they spread ;
Achilles lifts it to the fun'ral bed :
Then, while the body on the car they laid,
He groans, and calls on lov'd Patroclus' shade :

" If, in that gloom which never light must know,   740
The deeds of mortals touch the ghosts below ;
O friend ! forgive me, that I thus fulfil
(Restoring Hector) heaven's unquestion'd will.
The gifts the father gave, be ever thine,
To grace thy manes, and adorn thy shrine."   745
   He said, and, ent'ring, took his seat of state,
Where full before him rev'rend Priam sate :
To whom, compos'd, the godlike chief begun :
" Lo ! to thy pray'r restor'd, thy breathless son ;
Extended on the fun'ral couch he lies ;   750
And, soon as morning paints the eastern skies,
The sight is granted to thy longing eyes.
But now the peaceful hours of sacred night
Demand refection, and to rest invite :
Nor thou, O father ! thus consum'd with woe,   755
The common cares that nourish life forego.
Not thus did Niobe, of form divine,
A parent once, whose sorrows equall'd thine :
Six youthful sons, as many blooming maids,
In one sad day beheld the Stygian shades :   760
Those by Apollo's silver bow were slain,
These Cynthia's arrows stretch'd upon the plain.
So was her pride chastis'd by wrath divine,
Who match'd her own with bright Latona's line ;
But two the goddess, twelve the queen enjoy'd ;   765
Those boasted twelve th' avenging two destroy'd.
Steep'd in their blood, and in the dust outspread,
Nine days neglected lay expos'd the dead ;
None by to weep them, to inhume them none
(For Jove had turn'd the nation all to stone) ;   770
The gods themselves, at length, relenting, gave
Th' unhappy race the honours of a grave.
Herself a rock (for such was heav'n's high will)

Thro' deserts wild now pours a weeping rill;
Where round the bed whence Acheloüs springs, 775
The wat'ry fairies dance in mazy rings:
There, high on Sipylus's shady brow,
She stands, her own sad monument of woe;
The rock for ever lasts, the tears for ever flow.
Such griefs, O king! have other parents known: 780
Remember theirs, and mitigate thy own.
The care of heav'n thy Hector has appear'd;
Nor shall he lie unwept and uninterr'd;
Soon may thy aged cheeks in tears be drown'd,
And all the eyes of Ilion stream around." 785
     He said, and, rising, chose the victim ewe
With silver fleece, which his attendants slew.
The limbs they sever from the reeking hide,
With skill prepare them, and in parts divide:
Each on the coals the sep'rate morsels lays, 790
And hasty snatches from the rising blaze.
With bread the glitt'ring canisters they load,
Which round the board Automedon bestow'd:
The chief himself to each his portion plac'd,
And each indulging shar'd in sweet repast. 795
When now the rage of hunger was repress'd,
The wond'ring hero eyes his royal guest;
No less the royal guest the hero eyes,
His godlike aspect and majestic size;
Here youthful grace and noble fire engage, 800
And there the mild benevolence of age.
Thus gazing long, the silence neither broke
(A solemn scene!); at length the father spoke:
     " Permit me now, belov'd of Jove, to steep
My careful temples in the dew of sleep: 805
For since the day that number'd with the dead
My hapless son, the dust has been my bed;

Soft sleep a stranger to my weeping eyes,
My only food, my sorrows and my sighs!
Till now, encourag'd by the grace you give,   810
I share thy banquet, and consent to live."
    With that, Achilles bade prepare the bed,
With purple soft and shaggy carpets spread;
Forth, by the flaming lights, they bend their way,
And place the couches, and the cov'rings lay.   815
Then he : "Now, father, sleep, but sleep not here,
Consult thy safety, and forgive my fear,
Lest any Argive (at this hour awake,
To ask our counsel or our orders take),
Approaching sudden to our open tent,   820
Perchance behold thee, and our grace prevent.
Should such report thy honour'd person here,
The king of men the ransom might defer.
But say with speed, if aught of thy desire
Remains unask'd, what time the rites require   825
T' inter thy Hector.   For, so long we stay
Our slaught'ring arm, and bid the hosts obey."
    "If then thy will permit," the monarch said,
"To finish all due honours to the dead,
This, of thy grace, accord : to thee are known   830
The fears of Ilion, clos'd within her town;
And at what distance from our walls aspire
The hills of Ide, and forests for the fire.
Nine days to vent our sorrows I request,
The tenth shall see the fun'ral and the feast;   835
The next, to raise his monument be giv'n;
The twelfth we war, if war be doom'd by heav'n!"
    "This thy request," replied the chief, "enjoy:
Till then our arms suspend the fall of Troy."
Then gave his hand at parting, to prevent   840
The old man's fears, and turn'd within the tent;

Where fair Briseïs, bright in blooming charms,
Expects her hero with desiring arms.
But in the porch the king and herald rest,
Sad dreams of care yet wand'ring in their breast.   845
   Now gods and men the gifts of sleep partake ;
Industrious Hermes only was awake,
The king's return revolving in his mind,
To pass the ramparts and the watch to blind.
The pow'r descending hover'd o'er his head,   850
And, " Sleep'st thou, father ? " (thus the vision said)
" Now dost thou sleep, when Hector is restor'd ?
Nor fear the Grecian foes or Grecian lord ?
Thy presence here should stern Atrides see,
Thy still-surviving sons may sue for thee ;   855
May offer all thy treasures yet contain,
To spare thy age ; and offer all in vain."
   Wak'd with the word, the trembling sire arose,
And rais'd his friend : the god before him goes :
He joins the mules, directs them with his hand,   860
And moves in silence thro' the hostile land.
When now to Xanthus' yellow stream they drove
(Xanthus, immortal progeny of Jove),
The winged deity forsook their view,
And in a moment to Olympus flew.   865
   Now shed Aurora round her saffron ray,
Sprung thro' the gates of light, and gave the day.
Charg'd with their mournful load, to Ilion go
The sage and king, majestically slow.
Cassandra first beholds, from Ilion's spire,   870
The sad procession of her hoary sire ;
Then, as the pensive pomp advanc'd more near
(Her breathless brother stretch'd upon the bier),
A show'r of tears o'erflows her beauteous eyes,
Alarming thus all Ilion with her cries :   875

"Turn here your steps, and here your eyes employ,
Ye wretched daughters and ye sons of Troy!
If e'er ye rush'd in crowds, with vast delight,
To hail your hero glorious from the fight;
Now meet him dead, and let your sorrows flow!   880
Your common triumph and your common woe."
    In thronging crowds they issue to the plains,
Nor man nor woman in the walls remains:
In ev'ry face the self-same grief is shown,
And Troy sends forth one universal groan.   885
At Scæa's gates, they meet the mourning wain,
Hang on the wheels, and grovel round the slain.
The wife and mother, frantic with despair,
Kiss his pale cheek, and rend their scatter'd hair;
Thus wildly wailing, at the gates they lay;   890
And there had sigh'd and sorrow'd out the day;
But godlike Priam from the chariot rose;
"Forbear," he cried, "this violence of woes;
First to the palace let the car proceed,
Then pour your boundless sorrows o'er the dead."   895
    The waves of people at his word divide;
Slow rolls the chariot thro' the following tide:
Ev'n to the palace the sad pomp they wait:
They weep, and place him on the bed of state.
A melancholy choir attend around,   900
With plaintive sighs and music's solemn sound:
Alternately they sing, alternate flow
Th' obedient tears, melodious in their woe;
While deeper sorrows groan from each full heart,
And nature speaks at ev'ry pause of art.   905
    First to the corse the weeping consort flew;
Around his neck her milk-white arms she threw:
And, "O my Hector! O my lord!" she cries,
"Snatch'd in thy bloom from these desiring eyes!

Thou to the dismal realms for ever gone !   910
And I abandon'd, desolate, alone !
An only son, once comfort of our pains,
Sad product now of hapless love, remains !
Never to manly age that son shall rise,
Or with encreasing graces glad my eyes ;   915
For Ilion now (her great defender slain)
Shall sink a smoking ruin on the plain.
Who now protects her wives with guardian care ?
Who saves her infants from the rage of war ?
Now hostile fleets must waft those infants o'er   920
(Those wives must wait 'em) to a foreign shore !
Thou too, my son ! to barb'rous climes shalt go,
The sad companion of thy mother's woe ;
Driv'n hence a slave before the victor's sword,
Condemn'd to toil for some inhuman lord :   925
Or else some Greek, whose father press'd the plain,
Or son, or brother, by great Hector slain,
In Hector's blood his vengeance shall enjoy,
And hurl thee headlong from the tow'rs of Troy.
For thy stern father never spar'd a foe :   930
Thence all these tears, and all this scene of woe !
Thence many evils his sad parents bore,
His parents many, but his consort more.
Why gav'st thou not to me thy dying hand ?
And why receiv'd not I thy last command ?   935
Some word thou would'st have spoke, which, sadly dear,
My soul might keep, or utter with a tear ;
Which never, never could be lost in air,
Fix'd in my heart, and oft repeated there !"
    Thus to her weeping maids she makes her moan :   940
Her weeping handmaids echo groan for groan.
    The mournful mother next sustains her part :
" O thou, the best, the dearest of my heart !

Of all my race thou most by heav'n approv'd,
And by th' immortals ev'n in death belov'd!   945
While all my other sons in barb'rous bands
Achilles bound, and sold to foreign lands,
This felt no chains, but went, a glorious ghost,
Free and a hero, to the Stygian coast.
Sentenc'd, 't is true, by his inhuman doom,   950
Thy noble corse was dragg'd around the tomb
(The tomb of him thy warlike arm had slain);
Ungen'rous insult, impotent and vain!
Yet glow'st thou fresh with ev'ry living grace,
No mark of pain, or violence of face;   955
Rosy and fair! as Phœbus' silver bow
Dismiss'd thee gently to the shades below!"
    Thus spoke the dame, and melted into tears.
Sad Helen next in pomp of grief appears:
Fast from the shining sluices of her eyes   960
Fall the round crystal drops, while thus she cries:
"Ah, dearest friend! in whom the gods had join'd
The mildest manners with the bravest mind!
Now twice ten years (unhappy years) are o'er
Since Páris brought me to the Trojan shore   965
(Oh had I perish'd, ere that form divine
Seduc'd this soft, this easy heart of mine!);
Yet was it ne'er my fate from thee to find
A deed ungentle, or a word unkind:
When others curs'd the auth'ress of their woe,   970
Thy pity check'd my sorrows in their flow:
If some proud brother ey'd me with disdain,
Or scornful sister with her sweeping train,
Thy gentle accents soften'd all my pain.
For thee I mourn; and mourn myself in thee,   975
The wretched source of all this misery!
The fate I caus'd, for ever I bemoan;

Sad Helen has no friend, now thou art gone!
Thro' Troy's wide streets abandon'd shall I roam,
In Troy deserted, as abhorr'd at home!" 980
 So spoke the fair, with sorrow-streaming eye:
Distressful beauty melts each stander-by;
On all around th' infectious sorrow grows;
But Priam check'd the torrent as it rose:
"Perform, ye Trojans! what the rites require, 985
And fell the forests for a fun'ral pyre!
Twelve days nor foes nor secret ambush dread;
Achilles grants these honours to the dead."
 He spoke; and at his word the Trojan train
Their mules and oxen harness to the wain, 990
Pour thro' the gates, and, fell'd from Ida's crown,
Roll back the gather'd forests to the town.
These toils continue nine succeeding days,
And high in air a sylvan structure raise.
But when the tenth fair morn began to shine, 995
Forth to the pile was borne the man divine,
And plac'd aloft: while all, with streaming eyes,
Beheld the flames and rolling smokes arise.
 Soon as Aurora, daughter of the dawn,
With rosy lustre streak'd the dewy lawn, 1000
Again the mournful crowds surround the pyre,
And quench with wine the yet-remaining fire.
The snowy bones his friends and brothers place
(With tears collected) in a golden vase;
The golden vase in purple palls they roll'd, 1005
Of softest texture and inwrought with gold.
Last, o'er the urn the sacred earth they spread,
And rais'd the tomb, memorial of the dead
(Strong guards and spies, till all the rites were done,
Watch'd from the rising to the setting sun). 1010
All Troy then moves to Priam's court again,

A solemn, silent, melancholy train :
Assembled there, from pious toil they rest,
And sadly shar'd the last sepulchral feast.
  Such honours Ilion to her hero paid,   1015
And peaceful slept the mighty Hector's shade.

THE WORLD

ACCORDING TO

HOMER.

THE TROAD

AND THE

HELLESPONT.

NOTES.

Iliad: poem about Ilios, or Ilion (Troy). Cf. *Æneid*, poem about Æneas. Similarly, what is the meaning of Pope's *Dunciad?* Some critics have claimed that the *Iliad* might better be called an *Achilleid*, or that it was originally such. Cf. note on 1, below.

BOOK I.

1. **Achilles' wrath**: note the significance of the position. In the original, the Greek word for *wrath* stands first. Cf. the beginning of the *Odyssey*, "The man, O Muse, tell me about"; of the *Æneid*, "Arms and the man I sing"; of *Paradise Lost*, "Of man's first disobedience, and the fruit | Of that forbidden tree . . . | Sing, heavenly Muse."

2. **unnumber'd, heav'nly**: observe the mark of elision. This was commonly used in Pope's time, even in prose. Even such forms as *reply'd* were common; but the elided form is not retained in this edition in words where the substitution of the elided letter would result in an incorrect form.

   goddess: cf. 9.

3. **Pluto**: Greek Hades,[1] god of the underworld, the place of departed spirits and not merely of the wicked.

   reign: used in what sense?

5. **unburied**: it was believed that the souls of those whose bodies had not been buried must wander on the hither side of the Styx.

7. **Atrides**: Agamemnon, son of Atreus; the termination *-ides* signifying *son of.* Who else might be called Atrides?

   strove: the strife is described below; this was the beginning of the "wrath."

8. Cf. with other verses, as to number of feet; and observe the usual metre of the poem. Alexandrines (iambic hexameters) are comparatively few in Pope.

---

[1] Hā'-dēs.

10. **pow'r**: cf. 61.

11. **Latona's son**: Apollo. Latona is the Latin form of the Greek Leto. Beginning with this verse, the Muse is supposed to tell the story, in answer to the poet's invocation.

13. **king of men**: a common epithet of Agamemnon.

15. **Chryses**: the "rev'rend priest" (13).

18. **ensigns**: defined in 20.

20. Homer's Chryses comes "bearing in his hands the fillet of the far-darting Apollo upon a golden sceptre."[1] "The woollen fillet wound round a staff was at all periods of Greek history the mark of the suppliant." (Leaf.)

22. **brother-kings**: Agamemnon and Menelaüs.

28. **Chryseïs**: the termination *-is* signifies *daughter of;* hence Chryseïs = daughter of Chryses. Homer knows her only by her patronymic.

30. **Phœbus**: the *Bright;* a very frequent epithet of Apollo, which came to be used as a proper noun. Homer generally joins Phœbus Apollo, but he has also Phœbus used alone. Cf. Phœbe, the fem. form.

32. **the fair**: of course, this expression is Pope's, not Homer's.

35. **fly**: how used? Cf. *sing* (2).

37. Cf. 20, and the note.

43. **labours of the loom**: weaving was the principal occupation of female slaves.

45. **Argos**: the Peloponnesus,[2] and not the city of that name.

49. **not**: some read "nor."

53. **Smintheus**: probably mouse-killer, from a word meaning mouse, applied to Apollo as the averter of the plague of field-mice.

54–56. **Cilla, Chrysa**: towns of the Troad.
Tenedos: the neighboring island.

55. **Thou source of light**: i.e. the sun; cf. note on Phœbus (30). If Phœbus means the sun, what does Phœbe mean?

56. **Chrysa**: cf. the forms *Chryses* (15) and *Chryseïs* (28).

59. **shafts**: the effects of Apollo's arrows are shown in 63 ff.

66. **around**: some read "about."

72. **pyres**: suggests the method by which the Homeric Greeks disposed of their dead.

73. **ere**: the early editions have *e'er ;* cf. the use of "ever" in Eccl. xii. 6, "or ever the silver cord be loosed."

---

[1] The translations quoted in the notes are frequently taken from the version by Messrs. Lang, Leaf, and Myers, without special mention in each case.

[2] Pĕl-ō-pŏn-nē'-sus.

74. **Juno (Hera)** : the sister and wife of Jupiter (Zeus).

Thetis : daughter of Nereus,[1] wife of Peleus, mother of Achilles.

76. **her heroes** : why hers? Cf. 725.

81–82. **spare — war** : observe the rhyme of this couplet, and cf. 119–120, 127-8, and others. In the matter of pronunciation, Pope's age was in a transitional state. It is impossible in many cases to determine what was the correct pronunciation of a word, or even whether there was a fixed pronunciation of it.

88. **hecatomb** : properly a hecatomb is an offering of a hundred oxen; but even in Homer it signifies a great public sacrifice, without regard to the number or kind of animals slain.

107. **Pelides** : cf. 7, note.

117. **blameless** : Pope, commenting on the great propriety of Homer's use of the epithet in this passage, says : " It is not only applied to a priest, but to one who being conscious of the truth, prepares with an honest boldness to discover it." Pope is not always so careful as he is here to follow Homer's use of epithets, omitting or adding them apparently wherever the exigencies of his verse require either.

123–4. **king — send** : observe the form of the verb.

124. **black-e'yd** : Homer does not tell us the color of her eyes, but calls her *quick-glancing* or *bright-eyed*, referring to the sparkle of youth. Pope applies this epithet in another place (246) to Briseïs, where Homer calls her *fair-cheeked*. Cf. note on 117.

131–4. According to later tradition, when the Greeks were collected at Aulis ready to sail for Troy, an accident brought upon them the disfavor of Artemis (Diana) ; and it was Calchas who at that time declared that the goddess could be appeased only by the sacrifice of Agamemnon's daughter, Iphigenia.[2] Some have seen in these words of Agamemnon a reference to that episode. However, as Homer nowhere else knows of Iphigenia's sacrifice, it is unsafe to assume a reference to it here.

143. **Clytaemnestra** : wife of Agamemnon.

175. **Or — or** : either — or.

177-8. Agamemnon is especially offensive in thus declaring absolute authority over the three mightiest chiefs of the army: Achilles, the greatest of all; Ajax, son of Telamon, mightiest next to Achilles; and the wise Ulysses, hero of the *Odyssey*.

187. **Creta's king** : Idomeneus.

198. **form an ambush** : this was regarded as one of the most danger-

---

[1] Nē'-reūs.

[2] Iph-i-ge-nī'-a.

ous, and therefore one of the most honorable, duties that the soldier could perform. Cf. 299.

204. **reign**: cf. 3.

209. **nations**: is this term properly applied to the Grecian tribes?

215-6. A sentiment entirely foreign to Homer; one of many such that Pope introduces.

221-4. Homer's Achilles says: "Now will I depart to Phthia, seeing it is far better to return home on my beaked ships; nor am I minded here in dishonour to draw thee thy fill of riches and wealth."

228. The royal power had its source in Zeus; kings are frequently called Zeus-nurtered. See also 369. Was Agamemnon's boast, made in this line, fulfilled by subsequent events? See summary of the *Iliad* in the Introduction.

239. **Myrmidons**: the subjects of Achilles.

265. **confess'd**: revealed. The gods sometimes appeared thus to individuals, unseen by all except the one by whom they wished to be seen.

294. **senate**: does this word accurately express the idea?

309. **this sacred sceptre**: the sceptre that had been placed in his hand by a herald, in token of his right to "the floor." The sceptre was the common emblem of authority; and so (314) "an ensign of the delegates of Jove" (i.e. of kings).

330. **Pylian**: from Pylos.

336. **example**: a predicate noun, not the subject.

341-2. These two lines explain what previous word?

347-350. **Pirithoüs**: King of the Lapithæ,[1] a sturdy mountain race of Thessaly, to which belonged **Dryas, Ceneus,** and **Polyphemus** (not the Sicilian monster). **Theseus,** King of Athens, was a friend to Pirithoüs, and his ally in the war between the Lapithæ and the Centaurs (357).

355-7. **boar — gore — tore**: observe three rhyming lines instead of the usual couplet, and cf. vi. 279-281, xxii. 63-65, and other examples.

363. Probably the division of spoil was made by the commander-in-chief in presence of the people and with their approval. Prizes of honor were given to the chiefs, and the rest of the plunder was a common possession of the army.

377. **awful**: cf. 277, and observe the accurate use of this word.

394. **secure**: explained by what follows in this verse and the next.

395. **in any woman's cause**: in Homer, "know that not by violence will I strive on account of the maid, neither with thee nor with any other." Pope's version seems to contain an allusion to Helen also, as the cause of the war.

---

[1] Lăp'-i-thae(-thē).

396. This sentiment is not in Homer; is it true?

402. **Patroclus**: the close friend of Achilles. See synopsis of Bk. xvi. ff. in the Introduction.

410. Here the poet turns to another scene, which fills the time while the embassy is on the way to Chrysa.

460–1. **since — doom**: Achilles had been given the choice of a long, inglorious life or a brief career full of honor.

464. **Thund'rer**: Zeus, hurler of the thunderbolt.

468. **in**: some read "from."

469. **aged Ocean**: Homer says "her aged sire," though he nowhere names him; known to later mythology as Nereus.

478. **Thebe**: one of the numerous smaller towns of the Troad. Cf. vi. 524–5. Perhaps sacked on the same expedition as Chrysa.

479. **Eëtion**: Andromache's father. Some early editions incorrectly spell Aëtion.

515–529. This legend is nowhere else referred to, either in Homer or other sources.

518–519. What three gods?

525. Homer says, "for he is mightier even than his father," Poseidon (Neptune), who is sometimes called the earth-shaker.

555. **warm limits**: in what direction? "Zeus went to Oceanus," says Homer. What is the Homeric conception of Ocean?

573. **fane**: "to the altar," in Homer, who has no temple in mind.

600–617. The ceremony was about as follows: first, the salted barley grains were sprinkled upon the fire of the altar (not between the horns of the animal, as was formerly thought); then the head of the victim was drawn back, apparently to make it easier to cut the throat. When slain, the animal was flayed, slices from the thighs (or, more probably, parts of the thigh-bone) were enclosed in double layers of fat, and the whole covered with choice bits from the rest of the body. These were burned on wood, while a libation of wine was poured over them. All this constituted the portion of the gods, who were supposed to enjoy the ascending savor. The rest of the meat was carefully roasted, and furnished a feast for the men.

609. **instruments**: five-tined flesh-hooks, shaped somewhat like a half-open hand with the fingers apart.

640–3. Cf. 554–9.

663. **counsels**: early editions have "councils."

683–7. Literally: " Kronion [i.e. the son of Kronos] spoke, and bowed his dark brow, and the ambrosial locks waved from the king's immortal head; and he made great Olympus shake." The description in these lines is said to have furnished Phidias the model for his famous chryselephantine statue of Zeus at Olympia.

713. "Hera the ox-eyed," Homer calls her.

714. **Saturnius:** son of Saturn (Kronos).

719. **consult:** observe both the use and the accent of this word.

731. **what is,** etc.: Pope's philosophy, not Homer's.

741. **architect divine:** cf. 779.

753. **double bowl:** Pope appears to have thought of this as a bowl shaped somewhat like an hour-glass, with a cup at each end; and so others have explained it. Perhaps, however, Homer meant a two-handled cup.

765. **Sinthians:** the early inhabitants of the isle of Lemnos. Pope uses this form for "Sintians."

770. Hephæstus was lame.

773. **ambrosial:** ambrosia was the peculiar food of the gods, as nectar was their drink.

BOOK VI.

1. In the Fifth Book, the gods have been taking part in the battle on the plain; now they have left the field.

5. **streams:** Homer here names Simoïs and Xanthus; of the latter he says in Bk. xx, "whom gods call Xanthus, and men Scamander."

7. **Ajax:** there are two Greek chiefs of this name, one the son of Telamon, the other of Oïleus; the Telamonian Ajax, as the greater, is always meant by Homer, when no distinguishing epithet is used.

9. **falchion:** the subject of *found* and *hew'd*.

21. **Tydides:** Diomed; cf. note on Atrides, i. 7.

25. **Euryalus:** an Argive. Of course, in the following contests, a Greek is always the victor.

28. **a fair Naiad:** "the fountain-nymph Abarbarea."

36. **sent to hell:** i.e. killed; Pope uses the word hell for the under-world; cf. note on Pluto, i. 3; also vi. 535, and the note.

38. **Nestor's son:** Antilochus.

42. **Satnio:** in Mysia.

46. **Spartan:** who was the Spartan?

49. **tamarisk's strong trunk:** Homer says, "stumbling (hindered, entangled) in a tamarisk's bough." The *Iliad* makes other mention of this shrub on the Trojan plain. It is common in modern Greece. It is not a large tree as Pope's expression might imply.

61. **told:** in what sense?

61–62. **brass, steel** : Homer says, " bronze, smithied iron."

85. **son of Mars** : i.e. soldier.

91. **Helenus** : one of Priam's sons.

99. **efforts** : observe the metrical accent.

108. **our mother** : Hecuba.

145. Observe the length of the shield.

160. Early in the Fifth Book, Athene says to Diomed : " I have taken from thine eyes the mist that erst was on them, that thou mayest well discern both god and man. Therefore, if any god come hither to make trial of thee, fight not thou face to face with any of the immortal gods ; save only if Aphrodite, daughter of Zeus, enter into the battle, her smite thou with the keen bronze."

191. **Æolian** : son of Æolus.

193. **Ephyre** : the ancient name of Corinth.

201. **Antea** : wife of Prœtus.

208. Prœtus, unwilling himself to violate the laws of hospitality by killing a guest, sends him to Antea's father, Iobates ; who likewise after entertaining Bellerophon, shrinks from slaying him, and sends him into perils which he expects to prove fatal.

210. **tablets** : this word suggests a knowledge of writing in the poet's time.

235–6. Homer says, " So when the king now knew that he was the brave offspring of a god."

242. Isander, Hippolochus, Laödamia.[1]

250. **fell by Phœbe's dart** : i.e. died a sudden, quiet death ; said of a *woman*. Cf. xxiv. 762; also xxiv. 761 and 956, where a similar death for a *man* is signified. Cf. note on next verse.

251. **by raging Mars was slain** : means simply "fell in battle."

252. **Solymæan** : Homer, "as he fought against the famed Solymi," ancient warlike inhabitants of Lycia.

257–260. Notable "instructions" : "to be ever the best and to excel all other men, nor put to shame the lineage of my fathers."

274. **Tyrian dye** : what color?

277–8. **when Thebe's wall**, etc.: referring to the famous expedition of the " Seven against Thebes." Distinguish between Thebes and Thebe.

291. Homer says, "Zeus took from Glaucus his wits."

293. **nine oxen** : there being no coined money at that time, cattle served as a measure of value; cf. Lat. word for "money," *pecunia* (from *pecus*, "cattle"), and its English derivatives; cf. also English *chattel* and *cattle*.

[1] Lä-od-a-mī'-a.

297. **Scæan gate**: the principal gate of the city, on the side toward the Grecian camp; thither had come the Trojan women to watch the conflict from the tower. Cf. note on xxiv. 886.

298. **beech-trees'**: the earliest edition has the plural form, and the use of the word "shades" suggests that this was in Pope's mind; though some editions give "beech-tree's." Homer says, "Now when Hector came to the Scæan gates and to the oak-tree." This tree is spoken of in the original as a familiar and definite landmark.

314. **Laodice**: Hecuba's daughter.

322. **the cup with Bacchus crown'd**: Homer simply, "honey-sweet wine."

329-333. Homer, "Bring me no honey-hearted wine, my lady mother, lest thou cripple me of my courage, and I be forgetful of my might."

334-7. Cf. Exod. xxx. 18-20.

362-3. **Sidon, Tyrian**: cf. I. Kings v., Acts xxvii. 3, Ezek. xxvii.

366. **veil**: "of these [her embroidered robes] Hecuba took one."

371. **Palladian dome**: house (temple) of Pallas Athene (Minerva).

awful: cf. the same word below (378) and elsewhere. See also note on i. 377.

394. **wond'rous**: observe the apostrophe; would it be used in this word in writing of the present day?

395. **full ten cubits**: Homer says, "eleven cubits long."

396-7. "before his face glittered the bronze spear-point, and a ring of gold ran round about it;" that is, where the head joined the shaft.

422-3. Cf. 399-401. How did Paris happen to be here at this time, instead of in the field?

466. **her second joy**: not, of course, her second child; she had but one (cf. 497). Homer says, "with her boy."

467. **Astyanax**: see note on 502.

470. **explore**: observe use.

491-2. **mourner — joyful fair**: observe the sudden change.

502. **Astyanax**: "city-king"; a name given to the boy in compliment to his father. In like manner, the son of Ajax is called Eurysakes,[1] "of the broad shield," and the son of Odysseus Telemachus,[2] "warring afar."

516. An interpolation by Pope.

524-543. Homer has been criticised for allowing Andromache here to give this long narrative of family history which must have been familiar to her husband; just as in i. 476-509, Achilles tells his mother the story of his humiliation, though he says to her it "is but to mention

---

[1] Eu-rỹs'-a-kēṣ.   [2] Te-lĕm'-a-chus.

what too well you know." In considering the force of this criticism, the reader should bear in mind the state of Andromache's feelings and of Achilles'; and the difference between narrating events, on the one hand, for the purpose of giving information, and on the other hand, reminding the hearer of one's sorrows as a basis for the prayer which follows.

528–533. Homer, "burnt him in his inlaid armour and raised a barrow over him; and all about were elm-trees planted by the mountain-nymphs, daughters of ægis-bearing Zeus."

535. **beheld the gates of hell**: Homer, "went within the house of Hades"; Hades, in Homer, always the name of the person (Pluto), its application to the place being later. Cf. notes on i. 3 and on vi. 36.

539. **Hippoplacia**: cf. Hippoplacus (495). Homer in the present passage says, "was queen beneath wooded Placus"; in the former, "in Thebe under Placus." Pope makes an error in spelling for Hypoplacia, the *Hypo-* being the Greek preposition meaning "under."

543. Cf. 250.

570. Belief in a Fate whose decrees were inexorable and inevitable was a marked feature of Greek religion.

583. Homer, "and bear water from fount Messeis or Hyperia," the former in Laconia, the latter in Thessaly. "The mention of these," suggests Mr. Leaf, "with Argos ('Argive looms,' 580) may indicate Menelaus of Sparta, Achilles of Thessaly, and Agamemnon of Argos, as the three probable masters of Andromache." The later tradition made her the prize of Neoptolemus,[1] son of Achilles. Cf. *Æneid* iii. 294 ff.

604–615. According to a story later than Homer, the Greeks, at the sack of Troy, hurled Astyanax from the walls; for Calchas had predicted, that if he lived, he would avenge his father's death.

617. Observe that while Hector *receives* the child from the nurse, he *restores* him to the mother, entrusting him to her care.

626–631. The idea of Fate again: this determined when he should die, and nothing could cause his death before the time decreed.

628. **to**: some read "of."

668. **contest**: for the use of this word, cf. next line.

676–9. Homer, "all this will we make good hereafter, if Zeus ever vouchsafe us to set before the heavenly gods that are for everlasting the cup of deliverance in our halls, when we have chased out of Troy-land the well-greaved Achaians."

---

[1] Nè-ŏp-tŏl'-e-mus.

BOOK XXII.

1. The preceding book closes with Achilles in pursuit of Apollo, who has assumed the form of the Trojan Agenor[1] in order to draw Achilles away from the field of battle, that the Trojans may have an opportunity to rush within the gates.

6. Pope, apparently, has in mind the Roman testudo; Homer says, "setting shields to shoulders."

30. Homer's Achilles says, "Verily I would avenge me on thee, had I but the power."

39. **Orion's dog**: the bright star Sirius, in the constellation *Canis major*, which took its name of Canis (Dog) from its proximity to the constellation of the hunter Orion. Sirius was supposed to exert an evil influence when he rose with the sun in summer, — the period that came to be named after him the "dog-days."

64. **mother**: Homer gives her name, Laöthoë, and that of her father, Altes. This passage seems to prove the existence of polygamy among the Trojans, though it does not show it to have been general among them; there is no similar indication regarding the Greeks.

69. **Lelegia's throne**: Homer says merely that her father gave her "much goods." In Bk. xxi., when Lycaon is begging Achilles to spare his life for a ransom, he speaks of "Altes who ruleth among the war-loving Lelĕges, holding steep Pedasus on the Satniœis." Cf. vi. 40–42.

71. Cf. note on i. 5.

112. Homer, "loosening the folds of her robe." The robe was fastened over the right shoulder by a brooch: this is what Hecuba unfastened.

122. **corse**: some read "corpse"; others, "corps."

140-1. When the Greeks were fighting for the dead body of Patroclus, Achilles appeared at the trench and shouted, frightening the Trojans. Then the latter held a council, in which Polydamas urged to retire within the walls for the night, while Hector favored camping on the field; and the latter's command was obeyed.

157. **terms**: those which Hector for the moment thinks of proposing are specified in the following lines, 158–163.

158. **treasure**: the treasure which Paris had carried away with Helen.

175. **The Pelian jav'lin**: Patroclus, when putting on the armor of Achilles (Bk. xvi.), "seized two strong lances that fitted his grasp, only

[1] A-gĕ'-nor.

he took not the spear of the noble son of Æacus, heavy, and huge, and stalwart, that none other of the Achaians could wield, but Achilles alone availed to wield it : even the ashen Pelian spear that Chiron gave to his father dear, from a peak of Pelion, to be the death of warriors."

178. **light'ning** : cf. wond'rous, vi. 394, and note.

189. **fore-right** : right to the fore.

194. **road** : perhaps a wagon-road encircling the city at a short distance from the wall.

201. **marble cistern** : in the original, "broad beautiful washing-troughs of stone."

241. **Tritonia** : Greek form "Tritogeneia," a word of doubtful origin ; epithet of Athene.

247–8. Homer, "yet scenting it out the hound runneth constantly until he find it."

251. **Dardan** : in the catalogue of the troops (Bk. ii.), the Dardanians are named next after the Trojans ; they are led by Æneas, and with him Archelŏchus and Acamas. *Dardania* (named from Dardănus) seems to be in Homer a wider designation than *Troja* (named from Tros, his grandson), and this wider than *Ilion* or *Ilios* (named from Ilus, son of Tros). The term Dardan is frequently equivalent to Trojan or Ilian. Cf. its use here with 314 and vi. 135.

276. **hell receives the weight** : a hyperbole symbolizing the fate of Hector.

284–6. According to the original, "No longer is it possible for him to escape us, not even though far-darting Apollo should travail sore, groveling before the Father, ægis-bearing Zeus."

291. **Deïphobus** : Hector's brother. This was a favorite way the Homeric gods had of deceiving men, — to assume the appearance and voice of some mortal, generally for the sake of securing their ends easily and simply.

311–312. **Or — Or** : how used ? Cf. i. 175, and the note.

317. **Enough** : not used as an interjection ; what does it modify ?

331. **Greece** : used (as often in Pope) in what sense ?

364. **dishonest** : for meaning, cf. next two verses.

370. **heav'nly** : is this epithet appropriate ? Why ?

391. **Jove's bird** : the eagle was sacred to Jove, as was the peacock to Juno, the dove to Venus, the owl to Minerva.

395. **fourfold cone** : "tossed his bright four-plated helm."

397. **Vulcanian frame** : cf. 370, "heav'nly shield."

405–6. In Bk. xviii., Achilles, lamenting to his mother, Thetis, the death of Patroclus, says, "and Hector that slew him hath stripped from

him the armour great and fair, a wonder to behold, that the gods gave
to Peleus."

421. **he**: who?

439-442. Homer, "not even should they bring ten or twenty fold
ransom and here weigh it out, and promise even more, not even were
Priam, son of Dardanus, to bid pay thy weight in gold."

451-2. As dying Patroclus (Bk. xvi.) foretells Hector's death, "verily
thou thyself art not long to live, . . . thou art to be subdued by the
hands of noble Achilles"; so here Hector dying foretells the doom of
Achilles. Cf. also Bk. xix., where Xanthos, the horse of Achilles,
prophesies, "nathless to thee thyself it is appointed to be slain in fight
by a god and by a man," to which Achilles replies, "Well know I of
myself that it is appointed me to perish here."

457-8. Homer says, the spirit (which is fem. in Greek) "wailing her
fate." Cf. note on "unburied" (i. 5); see also, 71 (in this book),
and observe the great anxiety of Hector to secure the rites of burial, in
his proposal to Achilles, 321-332, and his later appeal, 426-432. What
"dreary coast," then, does the poet have in mind in 457? Observe
how Hector's pleading for burial renders the following situation much
more pathetic.

467. **some, ignobler**: Homer says, "Nor did any stand by but
wounded him, and thus would many a man say looking toward his
neighbour: 'Go to, of a truth far easier to handle is Hector now than
when he burnt the ships with blazing fire.'"

494. "Great glory have we won; we have slain the noble Hector,
unto whom the Trojans prayed throughout their city, as he had been a
god." Cf. "Saul hath slain his thousands, and David his ten thousands." I. Sam. xviii. 7. For longer songs of triumph, see Exod. xv.,
Judges v., II. Sam. xxii.

502. **arms**: of which he had stripped Hector.

600-2. Jebb says of the Homeric woman: "On her head she sometimes wears a high, stiff coif, over the middle of which passes a many-
coloured twisted band, while a golden fillet glitters at the front. Either
from the coif, or directly from the crown of the head, a veil falls over
shoulders and back." Homer's statement here is, "From off her head
she shook the bright attiring thereof, frontlet and net and woven band,
and veil."

611. **Hippoplacia**: cf. note on vi. 539.

649. **Soft in down**: others read, "in soft down."

657 ff. "But verily all these will I consume with burning fire — to
thee no profit, since thou wilt never lie therein, yet that this be honour

to thee from the men and the women of Troy." It was thought that the disembodied spirits in Hades continued to follow the same occupations which had been theirs on earth. It was for this reason that with the body were burned the clothes, arms, and so on, which would be needed in the underworld.

BOOK XXIV.

1. **games**: the funeral games in honor of Patroclus described in Bk. xxiii.

34-35. "but the blessed gods," says Homer, "when they beheld him pitied him, and urged the clear-sighted Argeïphontes [1] [slayer of Argus ?] to steal the corpse away."

38. In prose, "E'er since that day" would follow "Troy."

38-41. Aristarchus rejected the corresponding lines in Homer as an interpolation. "The absolute silence," says Mr. Leaf, "as to the judgment of Paris, here alluded to, in all the rest of the Homeric poems, is sufficient proof that it is a purely post-Homeric legend." See the Introduction.

41. **Cyprian**: so called from the island where she was first worshipped.

56-57. Mr. Leaf, who states that this is an interpolation from the *Works and Days* of Hesiod, adds : "The Greek word expresses on the one hand, the respect for the opinion of men which we call sense of honour; on the other, it can stand for the wrong shame or want of proper boldness, such as prevents a man from properly doing his work in the world."

82. quire : observe the spelling.

94. will : cf. 144 and 145.

96. azure queen: why so called ?

103-4. **Between . . . Samos . . . and Imbrus**: Homer knows three islands by the name of Samos. Here he refers to what we know as Samothrace, while Pope understood him to mean the large island Samos off the west coast of Asia Minor.

112. **blue-haired**: cf. azure (96); both these expressions are Pope's, not Homer's.

115. **goddess of the painted bow**: Homer simply, "fleet-footed Iris": whence Pope's epithet ?

129-130. Homer, "and found the far-seeing son of Kronos, and round him sat gathered all the other blessed gods that are forever."

---

[1] Ar-ġe-i-phŏn'-tes.

141-2. Homer says, "Nine days hath dispute arisen," etc.

143. **Hermes:** Homer here does not name him, but calls him Argeïphontes, an epithet of uncertain origin, perhaps meaning Argus-slayer.

146. **glory:** as Mr. Leaf remarks, "The 'glory' accorded to Achilles is the receipt of gifts. If the body were stolen away and he received nothing for it, he would be disgraced; for it is in the receipt of gifts that the heroic point of honour lies."

195. **bow:** cf. 115.

245. **Phrygia . . . foreign regions:** i.e. at home and abroad.

249-250. **and wander o'er | Those hands:** cf. 588.

289-290. All this treasure seemed to the father too little ("too mean") in comparison with the priceless privilege of getting his son's body "back to Troy for one last look." Says Homer, "yet not that even did the old man grudge from his halls, for he was exceeding fain at heart to ransom his dear son."

311. **erring:** wandering from one to another.

337. Pope did not understand this passage of Homer. It was a "yoke-band" that was nine cubits long, used apparently to fasten the yoke to the end of the pole and also to a post at the front of the chariot itself; and so the length is not surprising, as it would be in the case of "traces." Likewise, the purpose of the "ring" (339) was not "the running reins to guide"; but this was a part of the yoke slipped over a peg on the pole to hold it more firmly. The passage in Homer is as follows: "The yoke they set firmly on the polished pole on the rest at the end thereof, and slipped the ring over the upright pin, which with three turns of the band they lashed to the knob."

343 and 345-6. Cf. 399-402, and 449.

361. **His winged messenger:** "the strong sov'reign of the plumy race" (363 and 383), "thy sacred bird" (382). Cf. note on xxii. 391.

390. Literally, "the dusky hunter called of men the Black Eagle."

393. **dexter:** cf. 364 and 384; the appearance of the bird on the right was a good omen.

417-420. Literally, "Straightway beneath his feet he bound on his fair sandals, golden, divine, that bare him over the wet sea and over the boundless land with the breathings of the wind."

421. **grasps the wand:** cf. 547 f.

428. **gray:** cf. xxii. 512.

430. **spring:** Homer says, "at the river"—the Scamander.

431. **Ilus' ancient marble:** literally, "the great barrow of Ilos."

495. Cf. Priam's failure to recognize Hermes and his fear at the latter's approach (441-4) with the closing words of Iris to him in 217-224, and with Priam's uncertainty regarding the outcome of his venture, 276-280.

530. err: is this a correct rhyme? Cf. note on i. 81-82.

547-8. Cf. 421-2.

553. Of fir: some read, "On firs."

606. see'st: cf. such forms as could'st, would'st, rememb'rance.

623. lay: what tense?

677-8. Cf. "His son," 572. In Bk. xix. Achilles speaks of his son Neoptolemus; but both passages in which allusion to such a son is made are suspected of being interpolations, agreeing with the later traditions about Neoptolemus. It is interesting to remember in this connection, that Alexander the Great claimed descent from Achilles through this son.

745. manes: dissyllabic; a word which Pope borrows from the Roman mythology; not used, of course, in Homer.

761-2. Cf. note on vi. 250.

762. Cynthia: so called from Mt. Cynthus on Delos, her birthplace. Homer does not use the epithet, but calls her here simply, "archer Artemis."

764-5. Niobe's boast was "that the goddess bare but twain but herself many children."

775. Acheloüs: a river of Lydia.

777. Sipylus: a mountain in Lydia.

816. not here: cf. 844.

820. open: others read, "open'd."

886. Scæa's gates: the word Scæan probably means left, hence (perhaps because the Greek bird-seer faced the north) western. Homer has no word Scæa. Cf. vi. 297, note.

900. melancholy choir: the professional mourners who lead the lament, while the women keep up an accompaniment of weeping; cf. 905, and observe the contrast between "nature" (those related to the dead) and "art" (the hired mourners). In Homer this passage reads, "and set beside him minstrels, leaders of the dirge, who wailed a mournful lay, while the women made moan with them"; cf. Jer. ix. 17-18. Cf. the form *choir* with *quire*, xxiv. 82.

929. Cf. note on vi. 604-615.

930-1. Literally, "For no light hand had thy father in the grievous fray. Therefore the folk lament him."

956. as: as if.

980. Cf. the lamentations of Andromache, Hecuba, and Helen with one another, and with David's lamentation over Saul and Jonathan, II. Sam. i. 17–27.

1015–16. Homer, " Thus held they funeral for Hector, tamer of horses."

PRONOUNCING VOCABULARY OF THE PROPER NAMES OCCURRING IN THE TEXT.

NOTE. — ae = e ; eu = ū ; oe = ē.

A-blē′-rus
Ăє′-a-mas
A-chā′-ian (-yan)
Ăch-e-lō′-us
A-chĭl′-lēş
A-drăs′-tus
Aē-ġē′-on
Aē-nē′-as
Aē-ō′-li-an
Aē-thĭ-ō′-pi-a
Ăg-a-mĕm′-non
Ăg′-a-thon
Ā′-jăx
Ăl′-çi-mus
A-lē′-ian (-yan)
Ăm′-a-zon
Ăn-drŏm′-a-chē
Ăn-tē′-a
Ăn-tē′-nor
Ăn′-ti-phon
A-pŏl′-lo
Ar-e-tā′-on
Ar′-gĭve
Ar′-gŏs
A-rĭs′-bē
Ăs-tŷ′-a-lus
Ăs-tŷ′-a-nax
Ā′-treūs
A-trī′-dēş
Au-rō′-ra

Au-tŏm′-e-don
Ăx′-y-lus

Băє′-chus
Bel-ler′-o-phon
Brī-ā′-re-us
Brī-sē′-is
Bū-cō′-li-on

Căl′-chas
Ca-lē′-si-us (si = shi)
Căs-săn′-dra
Çē′-neūs
Çĕn′-taurs
Chi-maē′-ra
Chrŷ′-sa
Chrŷ-sē′-is
Chrŷ′-sēş
Çi-lĭç′-i-an (-lĭsh′-)
Çĭl′-la
Clŷt-aĕm-nĕs′-tra
Crē′-ta
Çŷn′-thi-a
Çŷp′-ri-an

Dar′-dan
Dē-ĭph′-o-bus
Dī-ā′-na
Dĭ′-o-mĕd
Dĭ′-us

Drē′-sus
Drŷ′-as

E-ē′-ti-on
Ĕl′-a-tus
Ĕph′-y-rē
Eū-rŷ′-a-lus
Eū-rŷb′-a-tēş
Eū-rŷp′-y-lus

Grēēçe
Grēēk
Grē′-çian (-shan)
Glau′-cus

Hĕє′-tor
Hĕє′-ū-ba
Hĕl′-en
Hĕl′-e-nus
Hĕl′-lĕs-pont
Her′-mēş
Hĕs′-per
Hĭp-pŏl′-o-chus
Hĭp-pō-plā′-çi-a (ç = sh)
Hĭp-pō-plā′-cus
Hĭp-pŏth′-o-us
Hŷp-e-rī′-a (*in Pope*,
    Hy-pē′-ri-a)

Ĭ′-da

Ī-daē'-us
Īde
Ĭl'-i-an
Ĭl'-i-on
Ī'-lus
Ĭm'-brus
Ī'-ris

Jŏve
Jū'-nō

Lā-ŏd'-i-çē
Lā-ŏm'-e-don
La-tō'-na
Lē'-i-tus
Lĕl-ē'-ġi-a
Lĕm'-ni-an
Lĕs'-bos
Ly-çā'-on
Lȳç-i-a (ç = sh)
Lȳç-i-an (ç = sh)
Lȳ-çur'-gus

Marş
Me-lăn'-thi-us
Mĕs'-tor
Mi-nĕr'-va
Mūşe
Myr'-mĭ-don (Mĕr-)
Myr-mi-dō'-ni-an
Mȳs'-i-a (s = sh)

Nĕp'-tūne
Nĕs'-tor
Nī'-ō-bē
Nȳs'-sa

Oē'-neūs
Ō-lȳm'-pi-an
Ō-lym'-pus

Ō-phĕl'-ti-us (t = sh)
Ō-rī'-on

Pal-lā'-di-an
Păl'-las
Păm'-mon
Păr'-is
Pa-trō'-clus
Pĕd'-a-sus
Pē'-leūs
Pē'-li-an
Pe-lī'-dēş
Pĕrç'-nos
Phoē'-bē
Phoē'-bus
Phrȳġ'-i-a
Phrȳġ'-i-an
Phthī'-a (Thī'-a)
Phȳl'-a-çus
Pi-dȳ'-tēş
Pi-rīth'-ō-us
Plū'-tō
Pō-lī'-tēş
Po-lȳç'-tor
Po-lȳd'-a-mas
Pŏl'-y-dōre
Pŏl-y-phē'-mus
Pŏl-y-poē'-tēş
Prī'-am
Proē'-tus
Pȳ'-li-an

Sā'-mos
Sar-pē'-don
Săt'-ni-ō
Sa-tur'-ni-us
Sçaē'-a
Sçaē'-an
Sça-măn'-der
Sça-măn'-dri-us

Sī'-don
Sī-dō'-ni-an
Sĭn'-thi-anş
Sĭp'-y-lus
Sĭs'-y-phus
Smĭn'-theūs
Sŏl-y-maē'-an
Spar'-tan
Stȳġ'-i-an

Tăl-thȳb'-i-us
Tĕn'-e-dos
Teū'-çer
Teū'-thras
Thē-ā'-nō
Thē'-bē
Thē'-seūs
Thĕs-sā'-li-a
Thē'-tis
Thrăçe
Thrā'-çian (-shan)
Tī'-tan
Tri-tō'-ni-a
Trō'-i-lus
Trō'-jan
Troy
Tȳ'-deūs
Ty-dī'-dēş
Tȳr'-i-an

Ū-lȳs'-sēs

Vŭl'-çan
Vŭl-çā'-ni-an
Vē'-nus

Xăn'-thus (Zăn-)

www.ingramcontent.com/pod-product-compliance
Lightning Source LLC
Chambersburg PA
CBHW030556270326
41927CB00007B/949